GREAT MEALS DUTCH OVEN STYLE

GREAT MEALS
DUTCH OVEN STYLE

Dale Smith

CAXTON PRESS
Caldwell, Idaho
2004

© 2004 by Dale Smith

Library of Congress Cataloging-in-Publication Data

Smith, Dale, 1938-
  Great meals Dutch oven style / Dale Smith.
    p. cm.
  Includes index.
  ISBN 0-87004-439-7
  1. Dutch oven cookery. I. Title.
  TX840.D88S63 2004
  641.5'89--dc22
                                    2004008499

Kingsford charcoal bag in cover photo:

KINGSFORD® is a registered trademark of The Kingsford Products Company, Used with permission.

© 2003 The Kingsford Products Company. Reprinted with permission.

Lithographed and bound in the United States of America
Caxton Press
Caldwell, Idaho
171096

DEDICATION

I dedicate this book to you, the reader. Thanks for buying this book. I hope it will make your use of the camp Dutch oven a more enjoyable experience. It is also my hope you will benefit from it enough to share it with your friends.

CONTENTS

ACKNOWLEDGEMENTS

I would like to thank my friends and family for their support and family recipes that went into this book.

Specials thanks to my wife Alice for all the long hours of typing and correcting my spelling. Without her encouragement I believe this book would still be an idea in the making.

I want to acknowledge two of our close friends, Lorayn and Ron Robinson who spent so much time producing the cover photo, and other pictures.

And thanks to all those unnamed people who, over the years, have taught me so much about the Art of the Black Kettle.

INTRODUCTION

The reason I'm writing this book is simple. I became interested in Dutch oven cooking about twenty years ago. I spent many hours searching through book stores for a Dutch oven cookbook which would make my Dutch oven cooking easier. All I found, in any one book, was one or two ideas that were helpful. Most of the books I read only made me want to know more. Back to the bookstore I went looking for that one good book which would make the purchase worthwhile. That is when I started compiling my own recipes from my camping, hunting and backyard Dutch oven cooking experiences.

It is my belief a newcomer to Dutch oven cooking can, with a properly written cookbook, from the very beginning prepare good meals. A person need not wait twenty years to master the art of the black kettle.

In this book you won't find any old tired tales of how I fought off a grizzly bear with a Dutch oven lid or how the big one got away or nearly pulled me into the creek or how the pack mule ran off with the old grub box and we had to live on wild berries. While stories of this sort may add a woodsy twist to the book they add nothing to your education on how to prepare good meals with your camp Dutch oven.

I've worked as a professional baker for more than forty years. During that time, my hobbies were cooking, fishing, hunting, and white water rafting. It was on one such outing that I experienced my first meal from a camp Dutch oven. From that time I was hooked. I started with one 12-inch cast iron Dutch and now I need my pickup to carry all my Dutch oven gear.

Working at my career, food items and food ingredients became tools of my trade. Working with food every day, you learn and understand how different foods blend and mix with one another and how different spices and seasonings enhance different meals.

It's my intention for this book to show how anyone can master camp Dutch oven cooking and baking. It has been my experience any meal prepared in a home kitchen can be done equally as well on those hunting and fishing trips or in your own back yard. You can even build your own backyard Dutch oven pit.

Many people purchase a Dutch oven thinking about all the wonderful meals they can prepare only to find their use of the Dutch oven ends with stews or soups. In a short time, they put away the oven because they have reached their cooking limits. There is no reason anyone should fall into this rut.

During the early western migration, settlers were limited as to what they could carry. But one thing could be found on every wagon—a Dutch oven. The pioneers relied on the old black pots to cook every meal and they weren't limited to just stews and soups. They did all their baking in a Dutch oven. They also had to be creative so the meals did not become humdrum. (boring)

Today we live in a world where there is no end to the types of food we can cook in the Dutch. With all the ingredients, spices, meats, poultry and vegetables available, we can cook a different meal every day of the year. The secret is knowing how.

It is refreshing to step back into a time when planning and preparing wholesome meals occupied our thoughts. I'm reminded of the stories about my grandmother rising early with ten children to feed, using an old wood cook stove and nothing but primitive pots and pans, many of them cast iron, cooking the morning meal which, depending on the day, would consist of such wonderful things as biscuits and gravy, ham, sausage, bacon and eggs, homemade bread with fresh churned butter and the list goes on. Today that same morning meal might be orange juice, a cup of coffee and a health food bar.

Grandma would clear the table and after washing the dishes start the noon meal, which was called dinner. Then her attention turned to the evening meal we called supper. Supper was a repeat of dinner only with different foods. These meals included potatoes and gravy, fresh corn or fresh snapped green beans or shelled peas fresh from the garden. The aroma of roast beef or baked ham would come from the oven of that old wood stove. When fresh vegetables weren't in season, Grandma would go to her cellar and get a quart glass jar she had canned on that old wood stove. Of course, supper wouldn't be complete without one of her homemade pies.

By contrast, today our noon meal might be a burger and fries with a soft drink. Our evening meal could be a delivered pizza or something heated in a microwave.

I don't suggest we give up all our modern ways of eating, but there is a lot to be said for stepping back in time if only for a little while, and taking the time to fix a wholesome dinner for your family in that old black kettle we call the Dutch oven.

In selecting the recipes for this book, I've chosen my favorites. You will notice the names of each refer to what the meal is. I have prepared all the recipes in the Dutch oven so I know they will work if the directions are followed.

I will teach you how to adjust the coals or briquettes on top and bottom to achieve the proper results. The heat control is most important when it's applied to baking bread, rolls and cakes than any other time. I'm including a chart that will cover temperature ranging from 300 degrees to 450 degrees for the three most popular size Dutch ovens, 10-inch, 12-inch and 14-inch.

There is a section, *Fire In the Hole,* for those who seek a real adventure using your camp Dutch. You'll learn to cook and bake using natural wood coals in a pit in the ground and I've provided some special recipes for that purpose. I'm sure you'll enjoy them.

I believe if you will apply the rules of cooking and baking in this book, with practice you will be able to take any recipe from any book and prepare it in a Dutch with excellent results first and every time. I believe the principles in this book will prepare you to do just that.

If you're like me, when you go camping, hunting or on a fishing trip, you want your cooking to be easy but taste good. In this book you will find many recipes for one pot dinners that will provide you with a variety of good wholesome meals you will be proud to share with family and friends. The idea of cooking a complete meal in one pot is where the camp Dutch oven stands far above any other method of preparing meals.

It is my hope this book will help you enjoy many years of Dutch oven cooking.

INTERNATIONAL DUTCH OVEN SOCIETY

The International Dutch Oven Society (IDOS) is a non-profit organization based in Logan, Utah. Its primary mission is to promote and encourage the art and skill of Dutch oven cooking and to provide education regarding the benefits and methods of Dutch oven cooking.

Dick Michaud, Mike and Juanita Kohler and Ron Jones conceived the IDOS in 1984.

It was started after the Great American Dutch Oven Cookoff, in Logan had been held for five years with great success. The cookoff's name was changed in 1987 to the World Championship Dutch Oven Cookoff.

In 1990 the IDOS was officially registered in Utah with Dick Michaud as the society's original Executive Director.

There are IDOS members all over the United States, Canada and several other countries. There are more than sixty cookoffs in fifteen states. IDOS does not run cookoffs. It assists cookoff chairs with information on the do's and don'ts of having a successful cookoff. It offers classes and demos to promote Dutch oven cooking and friendship.

How to Run Quality Cookoffs

The very best way to have a quality cookoff is to have quality judging. Not everyone can judge a cookoff.

Judge's Qualifications:

The best Dutch Oven judges will have all the following qualifications.

1. Possess a wide knowledge of foods.
2. Have personal experience in many methods of food preparation.
3. Have personal ability to control the cooking process using fires and Dutch ovens.
4. Possess the ability to recognize and reward excellence.
5. Have a long-term food memory so the first pot is equally evaluated with the last pot.
6. Have an appreciation of the efforts and expertise used to produce the results.
7. Have the ability to set aside food preferences and prejudices by judging every presentation on the merits, not on personal dislike for certain types of foods such as spinach.

Judging Standards:

1. Look for dishes that are the best you have ever eaten.
2. Ask yourself, "Would I be proud to serve this to any of my guests?"
3. A winner should be a good example of all around quality, not just a gimmick.

Food Judging Procedures:

1. Presentation of the food should include appropriate garnish, serving containers, color, contrasts, harmony and edible decorations. Light and dark color contrasts are often very pleasing. The pots should be very clean and well-seasoned inside and outside. Reward the pleasant emphasis on the desirability of the food. Penalize gaudy garnishes that hide the food, or are not edible. Extra décor should not result in additional points or a higher placement.
2. Exterior inspection of the food for color symmetry of form, evenness of cooking, volume, surface character and aroma. Reward even cooking that results in a uniform color and surface texture such as the golden brown rolls with crisp crust and the evenly browned meat. Penalize spotty cooking, burned spots, raw, tough, soggy, brittle or crumbling results.

3. Internal inspection. Dig in and look at the bottom. Seek to discover areas that are raw, under cooked, burned, off color or tough. Reward pleasant aroma, uniform color, evenness of cooking, consistent texture and completeness of the cooking process. Penalize spotty cooking, burned or raw spots, streaks or lumps.

4. Taste. "The proof of the pudding is in the eating!" This is the most important factor in judging. As a judge you owe to the contestants a clear palate that has no lingering flavors from previous foods. A drink of water, a grape or a dry cracker may help remove lingering flavors such as pepper or chocolate. As a judge you should have a strong desire to taste this presentation, especially if you have just tasted many items that are similar. The ideal dish is food that tastes delicious. Reward pleasant use of spices, natural food flavor, evenness of cooking, chewability and aroma. A tip on aroma. When the food is in the mouth, breathe in through the mouth and out through the nose. The many aroma sensors in the nose will tell you a lot about the food. Penalize for toughness, off flavors, rancid oil from improperly seasoned cast iron, burned food, foreign objects, ash, flatness, unwanted lumps, spotty cooking cold spots, raw spots, missing ingredients, unnatural food colors and soggy crusts. Yes, use a thermometer to insure that cooking temperatures meet food safety guidelines. Hot food should be hot, above 150 degrees F. Cold foods should be cold, below 40 degrees.

Field Judging Procedures:

1. Spectator interaction: Team members should be willing to share cooking techniques and tips with the spectators. The main reason for Dutch oven cookoffs, after all, is to pass along the art of Dutch oven cooking. Reward good efforts at interaction with the spectators. Watch how the team members interact with the judges, and compare that to how they interact with the spectators.

2. Cleanliness is a major factor during the field-judging portion of the cookoff. Utensils, ovens, ingredients, prep areas and personal cleanliness should be watched. Reward the use of wash areas, table coverings, washing of hands and covering food items from contamination. This may be outdoor cooking, but cleanliness is still very important. Penalize the lack of cleanliness in

preparation and cooking areas, ovens, ingredients and hand washing.

3. Dutch oven techniques showing proper use of ovens, heat source, tools and utensils should be judged. Reward proper use of tools, heat source and ovens. Team members should know how to start charcoal briquettes. They should also be able to show proper fire use. Lack of these skills should be penalized.

4. Other areas that may be judged are promptness of registration, team dress and timely presentation to the judges.

These suggestions are presented to promote quality judging, fairness and encouragement of the art of Dutch oven cooking. Prepared by A. Glen Humpherys, Ph.D. Curator Director of Wheeler Historic Farm, Dutch oven instructor, contestant, judge and enthusiast. Special contributions were made by Gerry and Chauna Duffin and by Jeff Currier. They are all experienced Dutch oven cooks and successful contestants.

The above is reproduced from the web site of IDOS www.idos.com with permission from the International Dutch Oven Society.

If you're interested in joining IDOS, the dues are $15.00 per year.

Contact them at:

IDOS
41 East 400 North
#210
Logan, Utah 84321

My first trip to an International Dutch Oven Championship Cookoff

For years I wanted to go to a Dutch oven cookoff. Any cookoff would be fine. However, I would hear about one after the event or it would be held at a time or location I couldn't attend. Then I discovered there was to be the International Dutch Oven Championship Cookoff in Sandy, Utah, which is only 475 miles from where I live. It was being held in March, which meant I was able to get away, weather should be good, spring is a nice time to travel and because our son lived in Salt Lake we could see the grandchildren. I marked the time on the calendar and started making plans.

The day before we were to leave the weather turned bad and we had winds of 45 mph. I didn't want to pull a fifth wheel trailer in winds like that so figured we would put off leaving for a day. Woke up at 4 a.m. and the wind had stopped. It was calm so the trip was back on schedule. Woke up at 6 a.m. only to discover it was snowing and we had at least 1/2 inch and it was really coming down. Went back to sleep, woke up and had about 1 1/2 inches of snow. Decided we would wait another day. The sun came out and melted the snow so we decided to leave. So what if we are a few hours late in leaving from our original plans? We figured we would go as far as possible, stay the night and arrive the next day. To our surprise, the weather was rather nice and the roads were clear. Clear that is until we were reaching Salt Lake. The rain started and the closer we got the harder it rained. The rain was so heavy we couldn't see the lines on the road. Salt Lake had just built new roads for the Winter Olympics and I wasn't sure where I was going but we lucked out since it was Sunday night, traffic wasn't too bad.

It was about 10:30 at night and we pulled into the RV park and that is when the fun began. The security man assigned us a spot and as I stepped from my truck and the smell of burned rubber was overpowering. (This smell later proved to be a problem with my front brakes.) Anyone who camps in a RV park knows the fun in parking and trying to hook up when it is dark and it is pouring rain. I disconnected the truck, hooked up the electricity and water only to discover there was a problem with the sewer connection and we couldn't use it. By now it was close to midnight and I decided things would look better in the morning so we stayed the night.

The next morning they moved me to another spot about 40 feet away. However, I still had to disconnect, move and hook up once again mumbling the entire time. I still had a problem with my brakes that had to be taken care of as soon as possible. Thank goodness for cell phones. I remember when my wife suggested we get one I saw no need for it. After this trip I'll never be without one. Since my truck is under warranty, I called the garage and explained my problem. They said we could bring it in but they were so busy they weren't sure when they could get to it. We took it in and told them our problem and they said they would do the best they could. We decided to wait. What else could we do?

We called our son and told him our problem and that we would let him know what was happening. About noon the nice young man told us for the past 32,000 miles our front brakes were doing about 90 percent of the stopping. They took care of the problem and a short time later we were on our way. We went to see our son. The next morning my wife had things she wanted to do. After I dropped her off, I'm driving down the street and I hear a ding ding ding in the truck and at the same time my check gage light goes on and the oil pressure falls to zero.

I am thinking this is not the trip I had planned. I pulled to the side of the road, and with my trusty little cell phone, I called the garage and talked to the same nice young man who helped me before only now we are on a first-name basis. I was worried about the problem and what I was going to do. He assured me if the engine wasn't making a noise it probably wasn't anything serious, probably just a sensor and it wouldn't hurt to drive it. However, they were too busy to repair it now and would I bring it in first thing in the morning.

I had planned on doing some Dutch oven cooking for my kids, but with the snow they had and then the rain I didn't feel like standing in mud. I decided since there was cable I would watch television and soon discovered there had been problems in the park and our connection didn't work. The lady said she was sorry and offered to let us move to another location. I politely declined and all the way back to the fifth wheel I kept muttering I wish I had stayed home and never come to Utah.

The next morning we were at the garage when they opened. I went to my favorite seat by the coke machine and read again my favorite magazine *Motor Trend*. I talked to four or five people who came and went while I waited. I looked at all the new vehicles. After a coke, a candy bar and a bag of peanuts the nice young man informed me they found the problem and as he thought, it was a sensor. Not only that sensor but also the sensor on the fuel gauge. He said not to worry, everything was covered under warranty and they would repair it as soon as they got the parts. They had located the parts locally and they were on the way so it would be only a few hours and I would be on my way. I called my son and told him the problem. He came and picked me up and I spent the day with him as he made his service calls. Thanks to the cell phone I was able to keep in touch with the garage and finally got the truck back at closing time.

Every night we spent time with our son and his family. We had made plans to all go to the cookoff on Saturday. I had called to find out the time it started and it was my understanding they started at 9 a.m. Not wanting to be late and not sure where we were going I got up at 6 a.m. We picked up our kids and we arrived at the door at 8:45 only to learn it didn't open till 10 a.m. After everything that had happened to us during the week I figured this wouldn't be much better. I warned my wife and kids not to expect too much. I figured this was probably a wasted trip.

Then the doors opened and immediately I looked for the cookoff. What I saw was a total surprise. The teams were making the desserts first and watching them work was very impressive. I went from team to team to see and learn everything I could. You could ask them questions and they were willing to help. When the desserts were completed, a member of each team brought their dessert to the judging table. I was in awe and very impressed with what I saw. There were pies, cakes and cobblers and they were finished in a beautiful manner. Being a baker for forty years, I was impressed such deserts could be from a Dutch oven. Next came the bread items. Again I was amazed at what had been produced in a Dutch oven. Next came the main course. What can I say! They were just as impressive as the deserts and breads. Their imagination, the practice they must do, the hard work and the finished product was fantastic. In my mind they were all winners. All the spectators had in mind who they thought would win and were discussing among themselves their ideas of the dishes.

The judges were all very professional and took their job serious. They looked, they smelled, they touched and they tasted. Each judge tested each item from each team.

We spectators stood in envy because we couldn't taste. The teams were judged on other things also. How they interacted with the spectators and how clean they worked were other considerations.

I was highly impressed from the time we arrived till the time we left about 5 p.m. At no time was I disappointed in what we saw. The time passed all too quickly and it was time to leave. After the bad week, I felt renewed and up beat again. Thanks to a great group of people and those little black pots I left thinking about the next cookoff and making plans to attend.

It had been such a bad week. People have asked me if it was worth it and if I would do it over again.
My reply is "Yes, in a heartbeat."

If you're interested in attending a cookoff in your local area or anywhere, check the Internet www.idos.com for dates and places and check the IDOS section of this book for more information.

Good cooking from the Smith family.

Preparation

How to Season or Re-season a Dutch Oven

A Dutch oven must be seasoned before anything is cooked in it. The factory covers the Dutch oven with a preservative that must be washed off with mild dish washing soap and hot water. Dry the Dutch oven.

Line the bottom of your kitchen range oven with foil to catch any dripping from your Dutch oven while it is being seasoned. Heat the oven to 350 degrees. Now smear a *thin* coat of shortening, such as Crisco, over the entire Dutch oven and lid. The top, bottom, inside and outside. Make sure the entire surface is covered. Bake both the lid and Dutch oven upside down for three (3) hours. Shut off oven and leave Dutch oven and lid inside till it is cool to the touch. Your Dutch oven is now seasoned and ready to use.

After the Dutch oven is properly seasoned, it will have a golden color on the surface. As you use the Dutch the color will darken till it becomes black. As it darkens you will find the food sticks less and the Dutch will become easier to clean.

Should you ever fail to dry your Dutch thoroughly and rust appears use a wire brush or scouring pads to remove the rust then repeat the seasoning process. *Should anything happen to your original seasoning, be sure to re-season your Dutch.*

Cleaning and Storing your Dutch oven

After cooking in your Dutch oven, if any food sticks to the bottom or sides use a wood spoon or a plastic scraper to remove it. **Never** use a metal spoon or metal scraper. This will remove your seasoning. After the food is removed, wash the Dutch in hot water using mild dish washing soap. I suggest you go to a bakery or restaurant supply store and buy a good nylon gong brush, nothing will clean better without scratching. For those camping trips, you can also buy a restaurant busing pan, the kind used to clear dishes from a table. They are made of rugged plastic and just the right size to use as a dishpan for cleaning your Dutch.

Dry the Dutch immediately. If you have hot coals left or a fire near by, set the Dutch near the heat to insure all moisture is gone. Then store the Dutch in a dry area.

Some cooks tell you to spread a thin coat of salad oil inside and out before putting away the Dutch. If stored properly, this is not necessary. The problem you might have is if the Dutch is stored for some time, the salad oil will turn rancid and the Dutch will become gummy.

Remember: moisture can cause rust.

Do what is necessary to dry your Dutch and keep it dry. I have had my Dutch ovens for many years. I wash them thoroughly after each use and make sure they are dry and I have never had a rust problem. If you do get rust, clean the Dutch, re-season it and start over.

Store your Dutch oven in a clean dry area. Dutch oven storage bags are available. They come in different sizes to fit the Dutch oven. They are made of canvas with a zipper closure and canvas handles for easy handling. They can usually be purchased at the store where Dutch ovens are sold. They are well worth the price and I recommend them for storing and keeping your Dutch clean and dry.

Differences between modern style Dutch
and old style Dutch cooking & baking

I call Modern Style Dutch baking the use of a trivet and baking pans in the camp Dutch. Using the Dutch oven the same way a person would use a home kitchen range oven. Determine the temperature needed and set the temperature control to the desired temperature. Using the Modern Style, the Dutch oven needs to be preheated. An oven thermometer placed inside the Dutch will tell you when the desired temperature is reached.

When preheating the Dutch oven, coals on the top and bottom create the correct temperature.

For most baking and roasting the coals on top should be in a ring around the edge with 3 to 4 coals in the middle, as most of the heat travels down the outside of the Dutch. At the same time, to reach the desired temperature on the bottom, under the Dutch, place coals in a checkerboard pattern about 1/2 inch in from outside edge of Dutch.

The amount of coals on top and bottom of the Dutch will depend on the size of the Dutch used and what you are baking or roasting at the time. In this book is a chart to help you and it will become easier the more you cook.

I call Old Dutch Style baking the practice of placing the food directly in the bottom of a cold Dutch oven.
You place the cold Dutch on hot coals and place the pre-heated lid on top. Each recipe will tell how to pre-heat the lid and how many coals are to be used on top and bottom. This style of baking will take a little longer.

With both styles of baking more heat is needed on the top than bottom.

TIPS FOR BETTER BAKING AND COOKING
WITH A CAMP DUTCH OVEN

When you first set the lid on your Dutch oven, turn the lid a half turn to insure the lid seats well for a tight fit.

When baking or cooking, about every 15 minutes of cooking,

using a lid lifter, rotate the lid on the Dutch oven about a quarter of a turn. At the same time, also turn the entire Dutch about a quarter of a turn. This will help eliminate hot spots on both top and bottom heat.

Many Dutch oven cooks use a garbage can lid or a lid from a 50-gallon drum to set their Dutch oven on while cooking. Either will work but it is easier, for the cook, if the Dutch is at least 2 feet above ground level. I had a table made especially for Dutch oven cooking. It consists of a 3/8-inch piece of flat steel 17 inches wide and 32 1/2 inches long with a piece of 1-inch angle iron around the edge on four sides to prevent the coals from falling and it holds the ashes. On each bottom corner is welded a 1/2 inch threaded pipe stand.

Using 4 24-inch-long, 1/2-inch pipe for legs, I can screw them into the openings on the pipe stands and I have a portable Dutch oven cooking table. It also has a 6-inch high windbreak, which I purchased at a sport center, that was made to fit another gas fired camp cook stove of the same size. The windbreak keeps your coals from burning away on windy days. I do Dutch oven cooking year round.

There is an old saying, no one plans to fail, they just fail to plan. When planning a trip whether it is fishing, hunting or camping, I put a lot of thought into food preparation. I plan the meals and make a list of everything I will need. Whenever possible, I pre-measure the dry ingredients and put them in zip lock bags. I label the bags and store them in a box I take with me. As I put the items into the box, I mark the item off my list. When it comes time to cook, I'll have everything I need to prepare a good meal with no unpleasant surprises and the meals are always successful.

When it comes to baking, one of the best tips I can share is using Saf Brand instant dry yeast which is available in grocery stores. It comes in a one (1) pound vacuum packed foil bag. You use about 1/3 as much Saf yeast as you would use with any other brand. It can be mixed in with the rest of your dry ingredients such as salt, sugar and flour. Other yeast needs to be sprinkled over warm milk or water to dissolve. With Saf yeast this is not necessary.

Use *instant* powered milk in place of fresh milk with any yeast-raised product. Fresh milk needs scalding to change the enzymes. Instant powered milk can also be pre-measured to save you time. When you use instant powered milk, replace the fresh milk with 8 level tablespoons to 1-cup cold water.

After making either sourdough pancakes, breads or rolls, always hold back some dough or batter to mix into your sourdough starter. Let it set in a warm place covered overnight before you use it again.

If you're not going to use your sourdough starter for awhile keep it in a clean glass jar in the refrigerator. **Never store the starter in a metal container and never stir it with a metal spoon.**

The ideal temperature for any yeast raised dough right after it has been mixed is 80 degrees. If the dough is either too warm or too cold you will not get the best results. You should always cover the dough with a piece of plastic.

When adding water to any Dutch oven that is cooking, add hot water. **Never** add cold water to a hot Dutch oven. Cold water can crack the Dutch and by adding hot water, it will take less time for your Dutch to recover the desired temperature.

Always make sure your Dutch oven is setting level. Especially if you're going to sear meat, fry chicken or cook other meat where you use oil in the bottom of the Dutch. If the Dutch is not level the oil will run to the lowest side.

Never use a metal spoon when stirring in the Dutch. This can scrape the sides or bottom removing the seasoning. Always stir with a wooden spoon.

At the end of your cooking period, if you have a lot of good hot coals left and you don't want to waste them, put them is a metal can and place a lid on top. This will shut off the air and the coals will go out. The coals can be saved till later. Use these coals when the number of coals is not so important, such as in simmering. Simply re-light the coals and they will work just fine. You can usually buy a clean metal can with a lid at any paint store.

It is possible to cook in several Dutch ovens at the same time by stacking them on top of each other.

An example is:

It is possible to roast meat in a 14-inch Dutch that will take 2 to 3 hours and to bake cornbread at the same time. Place your cornbread in a 10-inch Dutch and stack it on top of the 14-inch Dutch. You need 7 coals under the 10-inch for the cornbread and 7 coals on top of the 14-inch. Then place 16 coals on top of the edge of the 10-inch Dutch. Both will bake at the same time. The cornbread will finish before the roast. Remove the cornbread and finish cooking the roast.

If you live in an area where you have access to hardwood, using natural wood coals will work well with your Dutch oven due to the long burning time hardwood will give you. If you only have access to pine, you will have better results by using charcoal briquettes. When buying briquettes, don't try to save money by using a cheaper brand. They burn faster and leave a lot of ash. Self-lighting briquettes have been saturated with fire starter and burn faster. The best way to light your coals is with a coal chimney and paper. Don't use flammable liquids.

To guarantee you're cooking your meat, whether it is beef, pork or poultry, to the correct temperature, use an oven thermometer. Insert it into the thickest part of the meat and you will know when the meat is done. This will prevent over cooking or under cooking.

After you have browned your meat, such as a roast, use a trivet for cooking the meat. The secret to a good pot roast, from a tough piece of meat, is liquid and heat. Always roast meat on a trivet with the water coming up only 1/2 inch on the sides of the roast. If you roast a piece of meat totally dry, the meat will be tough, as the connective tissue in the meat dries. However, if the meat is roasted with too much water, the connective tissue will break down and meat will fall apart. With the rule of using 1/2 inch water up the sides of the roast the roast will be tender and yet firm.

I have several different size Dutch ovens, an 8-inch, 10 inch, 12 inch, 12 inch deep and a 14-inch deep. I choose the size Dutch to accommodate what I am cooking. In this book, you will find I use all sizes.

There are several items I feel are necessary to successful and enjoyable cooking:

Good pair of oven mitts, welding mitts are a good example
Small level
Lid Holder
Lid lifter
Trivet
Oven thermometer
Meat thermometer
Pair of metal tongs (to be used for moving hot coals)
Pair of tongs (to be used for turning food in the Dutch)
Set of good sharp knives
Large bread board
Long handle basting brush
Most important is a Dutch cooking table (will save your back and
    knees)
Wooden spoon

**Always have enough hot coals ready
to maintain required heat.**

COOKING CHART

Temperature degree	10-in. Dutch top	bottom	12 in. Dutch top	bottom	14 in. Dutch top	bottom
300	12	5	14	7	15	9
325	13	6	15	7	17	9
350	14	6	16	8	18	10
375	15	6	17	9	19	11
400	16	7	18	9	21	11
425	17	7	19	10	22	12
450	18	8	21	10	23	12

The above chart is a very good starting point.

Remember, on windy days you may have to add 1 or more coals to maintain the temperature. It would also help to use a windscreen.

This chart is for using the 3 most popular used Dutch ovens, 10 inch, 12 inch and the 14 inch.

THE ART OF THE BLACK KETTLE

When talking to someone about a Dutch oven, if they have never used one, they might answer "A Dutch what? Is that a new cooking gadget?" No you say, this is an old cooking gadget.

A lot of people barbecue in their backyards. Almost everyone, at sometime in their life, perhaps in scouting, has roasted a wiener on a stick over an open fire, but many of the same folks will think you are out of your mind when you describe the black cast iron pot with its three little legs, then go on in great detail telling how this pot was responsible for settling the western half of these United States of America.

Perhaps that is not entirely correct; however, from time to time I wonder if it's not part truth. Suppose you had been a pioneer going west from Kansas City to Sacramento in a Conastoga wagon with a wife, four children and a dog. Let's say the trip will take five months and you must take only what the wagon will hold, and that would be 1,400 pounds. At three meals a day for six people, times 30 days in a month, for five months, that's cooking enough food for 2,700 people. A wiener on a stick couldn't do it. That is where the little black pot called the camp Dutch came to the rescue. Not one wagon traveling west was without the cast iron pot and pans. I don't know why but there is something about simmering meat in a cast iron pot that will tenderize the toughest piece. That's a fact.

A lot of people going west had little or no knowledge of cooking with a Dutch, they quickly learned. Miss Nancy Wellington was just such a person. She was born in Boston to a prominent family of social standing. Growing up in Boston with servants and maids her life was far removed from that of the pioneer woman who traveled west. She couldn't imagine her life except to continue and mirror that of a lady of her social standing. At such a social gathering she met Lieutenant Elijah Sellers, a Union Army officer. He had spent most of his Army career at Army forts in the west. He had come home after being discharged from the Army. Nancy and Elijah fell in love and soon they married. In the years that followed, Nancy gave birth to four children—two boys and two girls. Her social life continued and she continued to have a servant and a maid and she felt her life was complete and perfect.

Elijah tried his best to be satisfied working for Nancy's father, who owned a factory which produced enamelware. Elijah had a job in the office, which paid very well, and he was well liked by all that knew him. Elijah's thoughts would always go back to the time he spent in the army out west and yearned for a life of his own as the tales of gold being found in Sutter's Mill spread east. Elijah became restless and it was only a short time and Elijah, Nancy and their four children found themselves in the fifth wagon from the end of a long wagon train moving west.

The children were excited as each day brought a new adventure. Elijah's head was filled with the thought of adventure and the wealth in the gold fields of California. For Nancy, it was a totally different life style. She found each day was a struggle to keep a smile on her face as she did her best to tend and feed her family. She had no servant or maid to help her but she vowed to make the best of the situation. Each day Elijah would bring a rabbit or prairie chicken for their dinner. Through trial and error, and for the sake of her family, and through her own determination, she did learn to make the best of her situation. As the miles and weeks went by Nancy Sellers became more creative, and by the time the family arrived in California Nancy could proudly say, "I've mastered the art of the black kettle."

FIRE IN THE HOLE—
HOW TO COOK WITH A DUTCH OVEN IN THE GROUND
When you decide to try this method of cooking there are some rules to follow for a successful meal.

When building the fire remember hardwood burns hotter and your fire lasts longer but pinewood will also do a good job. Fill the pit with wood and pile it high enough so when the wood has burned down all that remains are red-hot coals. Make sure there are enough coals to fill the entire pit.

Have your Dutch oven loaded and ready for the pit. Use a shovel and remove half the hot coals and set them aside. Set your camp Dutch oven on the remaining hot coals in the hole, *making sure the lid is well seated on the Dutch.* Replace the hot coals you have removed back into the pit on top of the lid of the Dutch oven.

PREPARATION 19

The next step will be your choice on what to do. My choice is to set an old metal garbage can lid on the hot coals, on top of the Dutch. Next I shovel about 2 inches of soft dirt over the top of the garbage can lid.

Wait till the cooking time has passed according to the recipe. Remove the top dirt, then remove the garbage can lid. Use heavy-duty oven gloves to remove the Dutch oven from the coals, being careful not to move the lid or tilt the Dutch oven. Once the Dutch oven is out of the pit, remove the lid.

The other choice, which you may prefer, in place of the garbage can lid, use heavy aluminum foil and follow with 2 inches of soft dirt. I prefer the garbage can lid because I find it neater and cleaner.

After the meal is cooked and the Dutch oven is removed from the pit you're all set to enjoy some good old fashion Dutch oven cooking. This way of cooking can just as easily be done in a campground, or on a hunting or fishing trip. Here you dig a hole and line it with rocks. In the morning, build a fire, as described earlier. Put your afternoon meal in the Dutch and put the Dutch in the pit on top of the hot coals. Cover with coals and dirt. Take off for a few hours of fishing or hunting and come back to an enjoyable hot meal ready for you. When you're finished with your camp pit just fill the hole with dirt and tamp it down.

As for the backyard fire pit, after the coals and ashes are cold, remove them from the pit and you are ready for the next meal from that long list of recipes you will want to prepare with the Dutch oven style I call *Fire in the Hole*.

Basically, *Fire in the Hole* is similar to using a slow cooker or crock-pot in your kitchen. Therefore any recipe written for a slow cooker, or crock-pot, should work equally well if cooked as directed in the chapter called *Fire in the Hole*.

HOW TO BUILD A BACK YARD DUTCH OVEN FIRE PIT
For years when I was camping with friends or on a scout camping trip I would volunteer to show them how to cook a meal in a fire pit by digging a hole in the ground and lining it with rocks. I had so

many requests for this type of cooking, I decided to build a perma-
nent fire pit in by back yard so I could teach a friend at home and at
the same time prepare a good meal for my own family. I'm glad I did
because now I use it all the time.

I cleared an area in what we call our garden area close to our
woodpile. We had tamarack and pine but I also bought a cord of
apple and cherry wood, from the nearby orchards in the county. As I
have said in other parts of this book hardwood will make a hotter
fire and burns longer. If hardwood is not available in your area,
tamarack, pine and lodge pole pine will do just fine.

After I cleared an area for my fire pit, I dug a **round** hole with a
depth of 2 1/2 feet with a diameter of 3 feet (at the top) tapering the
hole so the bottom would be about 18 inches diameter. A friend of
mine had torn down a brick flower planter and was ready to haul
the bricks to dump. I salvaged the bricks to use as a liner inside the
fire pit.

I purchased a 50-pound bag of brick mortar at my local lumber-
yard. When I was ready to lay the brick I mixed the brick mortar so
it would be ready for the brick. I started across the bottom laying the
brick flat but separating the bricks by a space of 1/4 inch. Next with
a hand trowel I spread the mortar into the 1/4 inch cracks and over
the bricks until all the bricks were covered with at least 1/4 inch of
mortar to insure the bricks stay in place. Next you lay the bricks up
the side of the hole, again leaving a space of 1/4 inch between the
bricks which you fill with mortar. When you reach the last row of
bricks put a ring of mortar over the top. This will help secure the
bricks in place and give it a nice finished look. Next let the mortar
cure for a few days (at least 3 days, depending on the weather)
before your first fire. The fire pit is now ready to use.

The reason for using bricks is the heat from the fire is stored in
the bricks.

FIRE IN THE HOLE RECIPES

Back Country Pork Dinner

Use 12-inch **deep** Dutch oven

1 1/2 pounds lean pork roast cut into 1-inch cubes
6 red potatoes cut into cubes
4 carrots cut into 1-inch long pieces
1 medium yellow onion cut into quarters
1 (28 ounce) can whole tomatoes, quartered
2 cups water
1 tablespoon instant beef bouillon
1 teaspoon salt
1 teaspoon black pepper
1/2 teaspoon paprika

3 tablespoons cornstarch
1/4 cup water

In the Dutch, mix all vegetables and meat. Add seasonings, tomatoes and water. Mix together slowly as not to break the tomatoes.

Cook 4 hours as directed in the *Fire in the Hole* chapter.

When meat is done, remove 1 1/2 cups liquid and put into a baby Dutch or sauce pan. Bring to a boil.

Mix 1/4 cup water with the 3 tablespoons cornstarch. Use mixture to thicken the liquid. After mixture has thickened, slowly add to ingredients in 12-inch Dutch and stir to mix thoroughly. Ready to serve

Like all the *Fire in the Hole* recipes, you can leave to go fishing and come back to a hot delicious meal.

Barbecue Chicken in the Hole

Use 12-inch **deep** Dutch
Use a trivet

1 large frying chicken cut into 8 pieces
1 large onion sliced into thin rings and separated
2 teaspoons minced garlic
1 green bell pepper chopped
2 (10 3/4 ounce each) cans condensed tomato soup
4 tablespoons packed brown sugar
4 tablespoons vinegar
4 teaspoons prepared mustard
4 tablespoons worcestershire sauce
1/4 teaspoon tabasco Sauce
2 teaspoons ground fresh ginger root
1 cup water

Place chicken on trivet in Dutch.

Place onion rings over chicken pieces.

Mix together water and soup.

Mix together tabasco sauce, ginger root, mustard, vinegar, Worcestershire sauce, brown sugar and garlic. Add to water and tomato soup mixture and pour over chicken.

Cook for 4 hours as directed in *Fire in the Hole* chapter.

Barbecue Pork Sirloin Loin Steaks

Use 12-inch Dutch

4 Pork Sirloin steaks cut lengthwise
1 large yellow onion cut into rings and separated
1 large green bell pepper thinly sliced
2 large tomatoes sliced
1 tablespoon quick cooking tapioca
1/2 cup barbecue sauce
1/4 cup red wine
1/2 teaspoon salt
1/2 teaspoon black pepper
1/2 teaspoon cumin
1/2 teaspoon fresh minced garlic

In bottom of 12-inch Dutch arrange green pepper, onion and tomato. Sprinkle tapioca over vegetables. Place steaks on top of vegetables. In a bowl mix together barbecue sauce, wine, garlic,
cumin, salt and pepper. Pour over meat and vegetables. Cook for
4 hours as directed in *Fire in the Hole* chapter.

Desert Hole Chicken Stew

Use 12-inch **deep** Dutch

8 skinned chicken thighs
1 can cream of mushroom soup
Salt and pepper to taste
3 medium potatoes peeled and cut into cubes
2 medium onions cubed
1 (8 ounce) can tomato sauce
1 package dry onion soup mix
1 can whole kernel corn drained
3 cups water

Place chicken in bottom of Dutch. Add salt and pepper to taste.
Place onions, potatoes and corn over chicken. In separate pan
mix dry soup mix, tomato sauce, mushroom soup and water
together. Pour over chicken and cook 4 hours as directed in *Fire
in the Hole* chapter.

Desert Hole Supper

Use 12-inch **deep** Dutch
Use trivet

3 pound chuck roast cut into serving size pieces
1/2 cup flour
1 1/2 teaspoon salt
1/2 teaspoon black pepper
1 1/2 cups beef broth – if broth is unavailable use 1 1/2 cups water,
    omit the salt and use 3 beef bullion cubes
1 (15 ounce) can S & W stewed tomatoes
1 teaspoon worcestershire sauce
1 teaspoon minced garlic
1 bay leaf
1 teaspoon paprika
4 carrots sliced
4 small red potatoes sliced
2 onions chopped
1 stalk of celery sliced
Water

Place trivet in Dutch and lay meat on trivet. Mix together flour,
    salt, pepper, paprika, and garlic, then pour over meat. Add rest
    of ingredients. Pour beef broth over vegetables. Add additional
    water, as needed, to cover all ingredients. Cook 4 hours as
    directed in *Fire in the Hole* chapter.

Down Under Corned Beef and Cabbage with Vegetables

Use 12-inch **deep** Dutch
Use trivet

2 1/2 pounds corned
   beef brisket
2 medium yellow onions
   quartered
1 pound baby carrots
5 small red potatoes cut
   in half
1 small cabbage cut into
   wedges
6 whole cloves
2 teaspoons prepared
   mustard

2 teaspoons grated orange peel
1/4 cup packed brown sugar
1 cup apple juice
4 cups water

Trim off fat of brisket and place on trivet in Dutch. Arrange carrots, cabbage and potatoes around meat. Place cloves evenly among the vegetables. Mix together apple juice, brown sugar, water, orange peel and mustard and pour over meat and vegetables.

Cook 4 hours following directions in *Fire in the Hole* chapter.

Fireside Barbecue Pork Sirloin

Use 12-inch **deep** Dutch

6 pork sirloin steaks
1 tablespoon salad oil
1 1/2 cups ketchup
1 cup water
1/4 cup vinegar
1/4 cup worcestershire sauce
2 teaspoons salt
2 teaspoons chili powder
2 teaspoons paprika
1 teaspoon black pepper
1 teaspoon Accent
2 large onions sliced very thin

Coat steak with salad oil then sprinkle with paprika, salt, pepper,
  chili powder and accent. Place in Dutch. Mix water, vinegar,
  worcestershire sauce and ketchup. Pour over steaks and bake 4
  hours following directions in *Fire in the Hole* chapter.

Prairie Hole Dinner

Use 12-inch Dutch

2 1/2 pounds stew beef cut into 2 inch cubes
8 carrots cut into 2-inch pieces
2 onions cut into 8 wedges
1 (14 ounce) can Italian stewed tomatoes
1 (14 ounce) can whole tomatoes
3 medium white potatoes cut into chunks
1 stalk of celery sliced
2 tablespoons flour
Salt and pepper to taste
1/4 teaspoon thyme
1/4 teaspoon basil
1/4 teaspoon oregano
1 tablespoon worcestershire sauce

Place one-half of the vegetables in Dutch. Place meat on top of vegetables. Mix flour, salt, pepper and spices together and sprinkle over meat. Add remaining vegetables. Pour tomatoes and juice over meat and vegetables. Sprinkle worcestershire sauce over meat and vegetables. Cook 4 hours as directed in *Fire in the Hole* chapter.

Serve with French Bread.

You come back to camp after a long day of hunting and you're cold. All you need is a large bowl of this stew and a slice of French bread and who cares if you didn't get a shot. Tomorrow is another day and perhaps some left over stew.

Roast Chuck in the Deep

Use a 12-inch **deep** Dutch
Use a trivet

3 pounds boneless chuck roast
1 teaspoon salt
1/4 teaspoon pepper
2 medium yellow onions quartered
4 carrots cut into 2-inch lengths
2 stalks celery chopped
1 bay leaf
2 teaspoons vinegar
1 can stewed tomatoes
5 cups water
3 beef bouillon cubes
1 small cabbage cut into wedges
5 medium red potatoes cut in half

1/4 cup cold water
3 tablespoons cornstarch

Set trivet in Dutch and place meat on trivet. Sprinkle meat with
salt and pepper. Place cabbage, carrots, potatoes, onions and
celery around meat then add tomatoes and bay leaf. Dissolve
bouillon cubes in water and add vinegar. Pour over meat and
vegetables. Set lid on Dutch and cook 4 hours as directed in
Fire in the Hole chapter.

When meat is tender, remove 2 cups of liquid and pour into a baby
Dutch or sauce pan and bring to a boil.

Mix 1/4 cup cold water and 3 tablespoons cornstarch and use to
thicken liquid. Serve over meat.

This was my dad's favorite meal and what's not to like. Just read
the recipe.

Trails Whole Dinner

Use 12-inch **deep** Dutch
Use a trivet

1 1/2 pounds boneless chuck roast
1/2 teaspoon black pepper
1/2 teaspoon salt
2 teaspoons minced garlic
1/2 package dry onion soup mix
2 tablespoons worcestershire sauce
1 tablespoon A 1 steak sauce
3 carrots cut into 2-inch length
2 stalks of celery sliced
1 green bell pepper seeded and cut into rings
1 medium yellow onion cut into quarters
4 red potatoes cut into halves
1 cup tomato sauce
4 cups water

3 tablespoons cornstarch
1/4 cup cold water

Rub garlic into meat and sprinkle with salt, pepper and onion mix.
Place meat on trivet in Dutch. Place carrots, green peppers,
onions, potatoes and celery around meat. Mix together water,
tomato sauce, steak sauce, worcestershire sauce together and
pour around meat. Cook 4 hours following directions from *Fire
in the Hole* chapter.

When done, remove 2 cups liquid and place in baby Dutch or sauce
pan and bring to a boil. Mix cornstarch with 1/4 cup water and
use to thicken liquid and serve over meat.

I was taught to cook this by a 15-year-old Boy Scout at a Scout
camp on the Salmon River. It taught me kids also like good
food.

Trails End Beef Surprise

Use 12-inch **deep** Dutch

2 pounds beef stew meat cut into bite size pieces
1 bay leaf
1 tablespoon worcestershire sauce
2 large onions cut into 8 pieces
1 pound baby carrots
6 medium red potatoes cut into quarters
2 stalks celery cut into 2-inch pieces
2 (15 ounce each) cans of S & W stewed tomatoes original recipe
1 (15 ounce each) can of whole kernel corn – use liquid
1 (15 ounce each) can of green beans – use liquid
1 (15 ounce each) can of peas – use liquid
1 teaspoon minced garlic
2 beef bouillon cubes dissolved in water
1/4 teaspoon black pepper
1 teaspoon salt
1 teaspoon paprika
1 teaspoon brown sugar
water

Place all ingredients in Dutch and add enough water to just cover.
Set lid on Dutch and cook for 4 hours as directed in *Fire in the Hole* chapter.

Wagon Wheel Brisket

Use 12-inch Dutch
Use a trivet

2 1/2 pound lean corned beef brisket
3/4 cup red wine or beer
1 tablespoon dijon mustard
1/2 teaspoon dried thyme
1/4 teaspoon rosemary
1/2 teaspoon salt
1/2 teaspoon black pepper
1 bay leaf
3 teaspoons minced garlic
3 carrots cut into 2-inch pieces
1 large onion quartered
5 small red potatoes cut into halves
1/4 cup water
2 tablespoons quick cooking tapioca

Set trivet in Dutch and place meat on trivet. Place potatoes, onions
and carrots around brisket. Sprinkle tapioca over meat and vegetables. Mix wine and water together and add remaining ingredients. Pour over meat and vegetables. Cook 4 hours as directed
in *Fire in the Hole* chapter.

BEEF

Barbecue Hamburger on a Bun

Use 12-inch Dutch
Use 15 coals in checkerboard pattern on bottom

1/2 cup chopped onion
3 tablespoons granulated sugar
3 tablespoons prepared mustard
3 tablespoons worcestershire sauce
3 tablespoons apple cider vinegar
1/2 cup water
1 cup ketchup
3 pounds hamburger

Simmer water and onions till onions are soft. Add hamburger and
stir-fry till meat has lost redness. Add all remaining ingredients
and simmer until hamburger will hold together on a bun.

This is a quick and easy meal when you are hungry but too tired
to do a lot of cooking.

Beef Enchiladas

1/2 cup water
1 1/2 pound ground beef
2 medium yellow onions minced fine
1/4 teaspoon allspice
1 1/2 teaspoon chili powder
1/2 teaspoon minced garlic
1/2 teaspoon ground cumin
8 ounces grated sharp cheddar cheese
1 package corn tortillas
1 bunch chopped green onions (also use part of the green tops)

Use 14-inch Dutch oven
Use 18 coals on bottom

Brown ground beef halfway. Add 1/2 cup water. Stir and break up meat. When meat is brown drain off fat and water. Add 2 minced yellow onions. Stir. Add chili powder, garlic, cumin and allspice. Mix well and continue to cook until onions are clear. Remove mixture from Dutch and place in separate bowl to let cool. After mixture is cooled add chopped green onions and 4 ounces of the grated cheddar cheese. Gently mix together.

Set aside.

Use 14-inch Dutch
Use 8 coals on bottom in a checkerboard pattern
Ring lid with 16 coals

Wipe out the Dutch to use again. Set Dutch on hot coals. Using a good no stick cooking spray, spray both sides of the tortillas lightly. Place the tortilla in Dutch and fry both sides about 30 seconds each side. (Turn the tortilla several times per side) Set the tortillas aside. Heat in Dutch two (2) 28-ounce cans of either red or green chili enchilada sauce to about 130 degrees. Pour enchilada sauce into a bowl and keep warm. Next dip each tortilla into the warm enchilada sauce, making sure both sides are covered. Lay tortilla on flat surface and place a large spoonful of meat mixture in center. Roll up the tortilla and place in Dutch with seam side down. Repeat this process until the bottom of Dutch is covered. Pour extra sauce over tortillas and sprinkle top with grated cheese. Do not layer tortillas in Dutch. You may have to repeat this process again.

Place Dutch over 8 coals and place the lid with 16 coals on the edge for only a few minutes. After they are warm and the cheese is melted, they are ready to serve.

This is the meal if you crave the taste of old Mexico but can't afford a plane ticket.

Beef One Pot Meal

Use 12-inch Dutch oven
Use 8 coals on bottom in checkerboard pattern
Use 16 coals in a ring on lid

1 pound beef cut into small pieces
3 tablespoons vegetable cooking oil
1 teaspoon dried thyme
2 cubes beef bouillon
1/2 teaspoon minced garlic (optional)
1 green chopped bell pepper
1 cup chopped green onions
1 cup diced celery
1 tablespoon worchestershire sauce
1/2 cup dry sherry
1/2 pound sliced mushrooms
2 cups water
2/3 cup uncooked rice
salt and pepper to taste

Mix beef with thyme, salt and pepper. Set aside.

Heat 2 tablespoons oil in Dutch. Stir in green pepper, green
onions, celery and mushrooms. Cook until tender and remove
from Dutch.

Add remaining tablespoon oil to Dutch and stir in beef. Cook until
brown. Stir in water, wine, beef bouillon cubes and worchestershire sauce. Cover and simmer 30 minutes. Stir in rice and cook
30 minutes longer. (Until rice is tender) Stir in vegetables and
stir constantly until heated.

This recipe is exactly what the names indicates. It is a full meal
cooked in a pot. Use paper plates and plastic silverware and
what is left is a Dutch oven and serving spoon to wash.

Beef Stew

Use 14-inch Dutch
Use 10 coals on bottom in checkerboard pattern
Use 18 hot coals on edge of lid

2 to 3 pounds stew meat cut into bite-size pieces
1 large yellow onion cut and quartered
3 tablespoons oil
2 teaspoons minced garlic
1 bay leaf
1 tablespoon dried sweet basil
salt and pepper to taste
1/2 cup all purpose flour
1 (15 ounce) can stewed tomatoes
5 sliced carrots
5 medium white potatoes peeled and cubed
4 stalks sliced celery
1 can whole kernel corn
2 beef bouillon cubes

Roll meat in flour. Heat 3 tablespoons oil in Dutch, add meat to
   hot oil and brown stirring constantly to prevent burning. Once
   meat is brown add hot water to cover. Add bay leaf, basil, garlic
   and bouillon cubes place lid on Dutch and simmer 1 hour, or
   until meat is tender. Add all vegetables, salt and pepper to
   taste. Add enough hot water to cover completely. Simmer until
   vegetables are tender.

This is the king of the "One Pot Meals." Served with Ranch Bread
   or Baking Powder Biscuits a person couldn't ask for any thing
   more.

Beef Stroganoff

Use 12-inch Dutch
Use 15 hot coals in checkerboard pattern on bottom

1 pound steak tenderized and cut into small pieces
1 medium diced onion
butter
1 can cream of mushroom soup
salt and pepper to taste
1/2 pint sour cream
6 medium sliced mushrooms (optional)
salad oil

Sauté onion in butter and set onion aside.

Sear meat in small amount of hot oil. After meat is well browned,
add onion. Stir well. Add 1 can cream of mushroom soup. Add
salt and pepper to taste. Simmer 1 1/2 hours, stirring to prevent
scorching.

15 minutes before serving add 1/2 pint sour cream. Mix well. Fold
in mushrooms and simmer 15 minutes.

Serve over cooked rice or noodles.

This is a favorite of my wife and, of course, it's one of mine too.

Beef Tips and Rice

Use 12-inch Dutch
Use 9 hot coals on bottom in checkerboard pattern
Ring lid with 14 hot coals

3 pounds beef cut into small cubes
1/4 cup salad oil
1 medium diced onion
1/2 teaspoon cumin powder
3 cups water
3 tablespoons soy sauce
1 teaspoon minced garlic
1 1/2 teaspoon salt
1 1/2 teaspoon pepper
1 package brown gravy mix
1 cup water

Add oil to hot 12-inch Dutch oven. Add beef and sauté until brown. Add onions and sauté until onions are cooked clear. Add 3 cups hot water, cumin powder, soy sauce, garlic, salt and pepper. Simmer until meat is tender. (About 1 1/2 hours) Mix 1-cup cold water with gravy mix and pour into beef mixture. Simmer, stirring constantly until beef mixture thickens. Remove from heat and serve over cooked rice or homemade noodles.

The recipe for homemade noodles can found under the Miscellaneous section.

Boneless Beef Ribeye Roast

Use 14-inch Dutch
Use 10 coals in checkerboard pattern on bottom
Line edge of lid with 14 coals and 4 coals in middle
Thermometer
Trivet

6 to 8 pound boneless roast of ribeye
3 teaspoons minced garlic
1 1/2 teaspoons crushed thyme leaves
1 teaspoon black pepper
1 teaspoon onion powder
1 teaspoon salt
1 1/2 cups water

Trim most of the fat from roast. Rub garlic, thyme, onion powder,
    salt and pepper on roast. Place roast on a trivet in Dutch. Add
    1 1/2 cups water to Dutch. Insert meat thermometer into the
    thickest part of meat. Place Dutch over hot coals and place lid
    on Dutch. Cook until thermometer reaches 140 degrees for rare,
    160 degrees for medium and 170 degrees for well done. The
    roast will take 2 1/2 to 3 hours to cook.

Serve with Cranberry Salsa (recipe in Miscellaneous section) over
    meat.

This is a showcase roast for that special company or Sunday din-
    ner when you don't want to heat up the kitchen and you're tired
    of using the backyard barbecue.

Corned Beef with Cabbage and Vegetables

Use 12-inch Dutch oven
Use 8 coals on bottom in checkerboard pattern
Use 16 coals on lid in a ring
Trivet

1 4-pound corned beef
  brisket
3 pounds potatoes cut
  into quarters
1 12-ounce package baby
  carrots
1 bay leaf
1 tablespoon beef paste
  or 2 bullion cubes
4 cups water
1 small head of cabbage
  cut into quarters
10 small pearl onions
1/2 large yellow onion quartered
Salt and pepper to taste

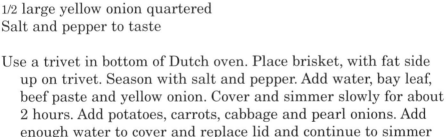

Use a trivet in bottom of Dutch oven. Place brisket, with fat side
  up on trivet. Season with salt and pepper. Add water, bay leaf,
  beef paste and yellow onion. Cover and simmer slowly for about
  2 hours. Add potatoes, carrots, cabbage and pearl onions. Add
  enough water to cover and replace lid and continue to simmer
  slowly until vegetables are tender, but firm.

Dutch Oven Spaghetti

Use 12-inch Dutch Oven
Use 16 coals in ring on lid
Use 8 coals in checkerboard pattern on bottom

1/2 pound uncooked spaghetti – break in thirds
1 large chopped onion
2 teaspoons minced garlic
1 pound lean ground beef
1/2 teaspoon oregano
1/2 teaspoon sweet basil
1 tablespoon salt
1/2 teaspoon fresh ground pepper
2 teaspoons dried parsley
2 (16 ounce each) cans tomato sauce
3 cups water

Brown meat and onion. Add all of the other ingredients, including uncooked spaghetti. Mix together well and simmer 20 to 25 minutes.

After cooking in your Dutch oven, if any food sticks to the bottom or sides, use a wood spoon or a plastic scraper to remove it. *Never* use a metal spoon or metal scraper. This will remove your seasoning.

Lumpias

Use 12-inch Dutch oven
Use 14 coals on bottom in checkerboard pattern.
No top heat

1 pound ground beef
1/2 head green cabbage chopped very fine
1 onion finely diced
2 whole carrots grated
Salt and pepper to taste
1 egg well beaten
1 package Lumpia wrappers (they are sold in Oriental food stores)
Salad oil

Brown meat in Dutch oven. Add cabbage, onions, carrots, salt and
pepper. Mix well and cook together for 1 minute, stirring constantly. Set aside and let mixture cool completely.
Put 1 heaping tablespoon of mixture on a Lumpia wrapper and
roll up into a firm roll. Wet edge with beaten egg to hold firm.
Wet ends with egg mixture and tuck inside roll. Press to get a
good seal. Set aside until ready to use.

Sauce
1/2 cup apple cider vinegar
1/2 cup soy sauce
1/2 cup onion chopped
1/2 cup green bell pepper chopped
1 teaspoon ground fresh ginger
1/2 cup water

Use an 8-inch Dutch
6 coals on bottom in checkerboard pattern

Boil all the ingredients, for the sauce, for a full 3 minutes. Remove
from heat and run through a strainer, keeping only the liquid.

The sauce can be made ahead of time. Put in an airtight container.
Placed in refrigeration it may be stored for at least 2 weeks.

Use an 8-inch Dutch

Use at least 8 coals on bottom.

Fry the Lumpia in about 1 1/2 inches of salad oil, turning so both sides are cooked. Remove from Dutch oven and place in a pan lined with paper towels to let drain.

Dip the Lumpia into the sauce as you are eating.

Pepper Steak Stir Fry

Use 12-inch Dutch oven
Use 15 coals on bottom
No top heat

2 tablespoons salad oil
1 pound sirloin steak cut into thin slices
2 scallions sliced thin (green onions)
1/2-cup celery sliced diagonally
1 large green bell pepper cut into thin strips
1/4 cup molasses
2 tablespoons soy sauce
1 teaspoon lemon juice
1/2 teaspoon hot red pepper sauce
1/2 teaspoon salt
1 teaspoon fresh grated ginger
1/2 cup cold water
2 teaspoons cornstarch

Heat oil in Dutch. Add beef and fry 5 minutes, stirring constantly. Add green pepper, onions and celery. Stir fry 3 to 5 minutes. Add molasses, soy sauce, lemon juice, ginger, pepper sauce and seasonings. Mix well.

Mix cornstarch in water and stir into beef mixture. Simmer until mixture thickens.

Serve over rice.

Round Steak In a Dutch Oven Meal

Use 10-inch Dutch oven
Use 6 coals on bottom in checkerboard pattern
Use 15 coals on lid

1 1/2 pound round steak cut into serving size pieces
1 tablespoon butter
1 onion sliced thin
4 tablespoons all purpose flour
1 1/2 cups warm water
Salt and pepper to taste

Sauté onions in butter. Remove from Dutch oven. Brown meat in Dutch oven, then remove meat. Place onions in Dutch and add 4 tablespoons flour, stir and add 1 1/2 cups water. Continue stirring to make gravy. Add meat, salt and pepper to mixture and simmer about 1 hour. Check frequently to make sure gravy isn't dry. If needed add more water. Serve with mashed or baked potato and a green salad.

Round Steak Sauerbraten

Use 12-inch Dutch oven
Use 9 coals on bottom in checkerboard pattern
Use 17 coals on lid

1 1/2 pound round steak cut into 1-inch squares
1 tablespoon salad oil
1 envelope brown gravy mix
2 cups warm water
1 tablespoon instant minced onion
2 tablespoons wine vinegar
2 tablespoons brown sugar
1/2 teaspoon salt
1/4 teaspoon pepper
1/2 teaspoon ginger
1 bay leaf

Brown meat in hot oil in Dutch. Remove meat. Add gravy mix and
warm water. Bring to a boil, stirring constantly. Add remaining
ingredients and meat. Cover and simmer about 1 1/2 hours. Stir
occasionally. **Remove** bay leaf. Serve over hot buttered noodles.

Savory Pepper Steak

Use 12-inch Dutch
Use 9 coals on bottom in checkerboard pattern
Use 17 coals on lid

1 1/2 pounds round steak cut into thin strips
1/4 cup flour
1/2 teaspoon salt
1/8 teaspoon pepper
1/4 cup salad oil
1 (15 ounce) can stewed tomatoes
1 1/2 teaspoon worcestershire sauce
1 3/4 cups warm water
1/2 cup chopped onion
1 small clove of garlic minced
1 tablespoon beef-flavor gravy base*
2 large green peppers cut in strips
Hot cooked rice

Coat meat with flour, salt and pepper and cook in hot oil until
brown on all sides. Drain tomatoes, saving the liquid. Add
water, tomato liquid, onion, garlic and gravy base to meat; cover
and simmer 1 1/4 hours, or until meat is tender. Stir in worch-
ester sauce and add pepper strips, cover and simmer another 5
minutes. Add drained tomatoes and simmer another 5 minutes.
Serve over hot rice.

* For gravy base add a boullion cube to water.

Savory Pot Roast

Use 14-inch Dutch
Trivet
Use 10 coals on bottom in checkerboard pattern
Use 18 coals to ring lid

3 to 4 pound boneless
    chuck roast
2 tablespoons all purpose flour
Salt and pepper to taste
1 clove of garlic crushed
5 whole peppercorns
5 whole cloves
1 to 2 bay leaves
1 tablespoon basil
1 large yellow onion quartered
1 cup celery chopped
2 (15 ounce each) cans stewed tomatoes
1 tablespoon beef paste or 3 beef bouillon cubes
2 tablespoons salad oil
5 small red potatoes cut in halves
2 1/2 cups small baby carrots
8 pearl onions
1/2 cup turnips minced

Roll meat in flour and pat into meat. Heat salad oil and brown
    meat, on all sides, in the Dutch oven. Remove meat, place trivet
    in Dutch, and put meat on trivet. Add enough water till water is
    at least 1/2 inch high on sides of roast. Add celery, yellow onion,
    turnips, tomatoes, garlic, peppercorns, cloves, beef paste, bay
    leaf, salt and pepper. Simmer very slowly for 2 hours. Add hot
    water as needed to maintain 1/2 inch water on sides of roast.

When meat is tender, remove 2 cups of liquid and strain;
    save for gravy.
Add potatoes, carrots and pearl onions and simmer about 30 min-
    utes or until vegetables are tender.

Gravy:
Use 8 inch Dutch

Use 6 to 8 coals on bottom

Put gravy liquid into 8 inch Dutch and bring to boil. Dissolve 2
    tablespoons of cornstarch in 1/4 cup of water. Very slowly,
    add cornstarch to boiling liquid, constantly stirring until
    gravy thickens.

When serving, spoon gravy over meat and also vegetables
    if desired.

This will be one of the best meals you have eaten.

Standing Rib Roast

Use 14-inch Dutch
Trivet
Meat thermometer
Use 10 coals on bottom in checkerboard pattern
Use 14 coals in ring and 4 coals in center of lid

6 to 8 pound roast with large bone removed
3 teaspoons fresh minced garlic
1 1/2 teaspoon dried crushed thyme leaves
1 teaspoon black pepper
1 teaspoon onion powder
Water

Trim fat from roast. Rub garlic, thyme leaves, onion powder and
    pepper into roast. Set roast on a trivet in Dutch. Insert meat
    thermometer in thickest portion. Add enough water until water
    is 1/2 inch high on sides of roast.

140 degrees for rare
160 degrees for medium
170 degrees for well done
Cooking time is about 2 1/2 to 3 hours.

Serve with Cranberry Sauce (for recipe see Miscellaneous section)

This is another showcase meal.

Swiss Steak With Vegetables

Use 12-inch Dutch
Use 8 coals on bottom in checkerboard pattern
Use 16 coals in ring on lid

2 pounds tenderized
    round steak cut into
    serving sizes
1/2 cup all purpose flour
1 1/2 teaspoons salt
1/2 teaspoon pepper
1/4 cup salad oil
1 teaspoon fresh minced
    garlic
2 cups pearl onions
1 red bell pepper diced
1 small yellow onions
    sliced
1 (10 1/2 ounce) can con-
    densed tomato soup
2 cups hot water
8 ounces baby carrots
6 baby red potatoes each cut in half
12 ounces fresh frozen peas

Pound flour into meat. Heat oil in Dutch oven. Add sliced onion
    and sauté until onions are cooked clear. Remove onions. Brown
    steaks on both sides. Add onions, soup, water and garlic.
    Simmer till meat is tender (about 1 hour) then add potatoes,
    carrots, pearl onions, red bell pepper, salt and pepper. Simmer
    until vegetables are tender. Add frozen peas and simmer 10
    minutes longer.

This is a different way of cooking Swiss steak, but what a differ-
    ence. With the vegetables, gravy and meat, all you need is bread
    for a complete meal.

Szechwan Beef Stir Fry

Use 12-inch Dutch oven
Use 20 coals on bottom in checkerboard pattern
No top heat

1 pound beef flank steak
2 tablespoons soy sauce
4 teaspoons Oriental dark roasted sesame oil (found in grocery
  store in Oriental section)
1 1/2 teaspoon granulated sugar
1 teaspoon cornstarch
2 cloves of garlic crushed
1 tablespoon fresh ginger minced
1/4 teaspoon dried red pepper pods crushed
1 small red bell pepper cut into 1-inch pieces
1 (8 ounce) package frozen baby corn thawed
1/2 pound pea pods julienne cut

Cut the steak lengthwise into 2 strips. Cut across the grain into
  1/8-inch thick strips.

Mix soy sauce, 2 teaspoons oil, sugar and cornstarch and stir into
  meat strips. Set aside.

Heat remaining 2 teaspoons oil in Dutch oven. Add garlic, pepper
  pods and ginger and cook 30 seconds. Add bell pepper and corn
  then stir fry 30 seconds. Remove vegetables from Dutch. Stir fry
  meat strips for 2 to 3 minutes. Add vegetables to meat and stir
  constantly until meat and vegetables are heated throughout.

Serve with white rice.

This is like having food from the Orient without going there.

Tenderloin Roast

Use 12-inch Dutch oven
Trivet
Meat thermometer
Use 20 coals on bottom in checkerboard pattern
Later use only 8 coals on bottom
Use 16 coals in ring on lid

3 pound center cut tenderloin clean, butterflied and tenderized
1 pound fresh spinach
2 shallots
2 tablespoons garlic minced
1 ounce olive oil
Salt and pepper to taste
1 1/2 cup hot water

Sauté spinach, shallots, garlic salt and pepper in olive oil till
    spinach is wilted. Place tenderloin on flat surface and place
    spinach mixture on 2/3 of steak and roll tenderloin and tie as
    you would a roast. This process may be done the day before.
    Refrigerate.

Using 20 coals on bottom heat the Dutch oven, add oil and sear
    the meat on all sides. Remove 12 coals. Place trivet in Dutch
    and place a meat thermometer in thickest portion of meat and
    place the meat on the trivet. Pour 1 1/2 cup hot water in bottom
    of Dutch. Place lid on Dutch and cook until done.

140 degrees for rare
160 degrees for medium
170 degrees for well done

This recipe is for that special dinner cooked outside at home. After
    this dish, you'll be using your gas barbecue less.

Yankee Chili

Use 12-inch Dutch oven
Use 8 coals on bottom in checkerboard pattern
Use 16 coals to ring lid
Maintain enough hot coals to simmer throughout cooking time.

2 pounds ground beef
2 medium onions chopped
3 cloves of garlic minced
1 (15 ounce) can stewed tomatoes
1 (15 ounce) can Hunts Special Tomato Sauce
4 to 6 cups hot water
3 tablespoons Mexican seasoning
2 rounded tablespoons chili powder
2 cups red beans
1 teaspoon salt
1 teaspoon pepper
2 teaspoons cumin powder
2 seeded Jalapeno peppers cook only till hot enough then remove

Sort and wash beans before using.
Heat Dutch to a high heat then brown ground beef. After beef is
    brown add onions and cook till onions are clear. Add rest of
    ingredients. Simmer till beans are done. Serve topped with
    chopped green onions and shredded cheddar cheese.

Cooking with Jalapeno peppers can be tricky. Wash the peppers
    and cut in half. Remove seeds. After chili has been simmering a
    few minutes, add Jalapeno peppers. Taste test often until you
    get the hot you want from the peppers. Once you have reached
    your desired taste, remove all the peppers. If you forget even
    one, the chili may be too hot for your taste.

The perfect bread for this chili is a Dutch oven full of Grandma's
    Country Cornbread found in the Bread Section. Doesn't get any
    better than chili and cornbread.

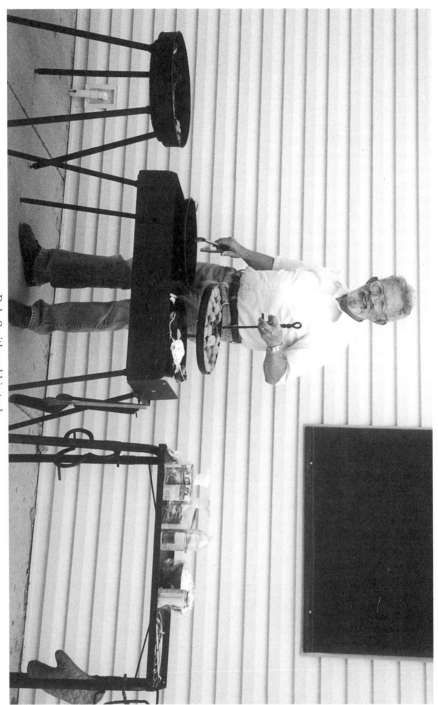

Dale Smith and his tools.

FISH

Cajun Shrimp

Use 12-inch Dutch
Use 15 hot coals on bottom in checkerboard pattern
(No top heat)

12 extra large shrimp – Take out veins and shell but leave on the
   tail
1/2 teaspoon thyme
1 clove of garlic crushed
1/8 teaspoon ground nutmeg
1/4 teaspoon ground red pepper (cayenne)
4 teaspoons olive oil
1 teaspoon paprika
1/4 teaspoon salt

In a small bowl mix paprika, thyme, salt, red pepper and nutmeg.

In Dutch heat oil till it is hot. Add garlic and cook 1 minute.
   Discard garlic. Add spice mixture and cook 30 seconds stirring
   constantly. Add shrimp, stirring to coat evenly with spices and
   cook 2 to 3 minutes or until shrimp are opaque (clear) throughout, stirring frequently.

Cajun Spiced Fish Fry

Use 12-inch Dutch
Use 15 hot coals on bottom in checkerboard pattern
(No top heat)

About 4 1/2 pounds white fish
6 tablespoons butter
2 lemons, cut into wedges
1 tablespoon Cajun spice

Melt butter in Dutch, add Cajun spice and heat thoroughly. Place
fish in Dutch and squeeze juice of 1 lemon into Dutch. Cook fish
for about 5 minutes, on each side.

Serve with remaining lemon wedges and pan drippings.

Corned White Fish

Use 12-inch Dutch
Use 15 hot coals on bottom in checkerboard pattern
(No top heat)

2 pounds white fish steaks
1/2 cup soy sauce
1 tablespoons water
2 teaspoons lemon juice
3 eggs
1/4 cup all purpose flour
1/2 cup rolled corn flake crumbs
1/4 cup salad oil

Lay fish in shallow bowl or pan. In a small bowl mix soy sauce,
water and lemon juice and pour over fish, turn fish over to coat
both sides. Marinate 5 minutes turning at least once.

In another small bowl, beat egg with the 2 tablespoons water.
In another small bowl mix flour and crumbs.
Remove fish from marinade, then dip in egg mixture then roll in
flour mixture.
Heat oil in Dutch. Fry fish in hot oil about 3 to 4 minutes
each side.

Fish Fillets Cooked in a Package ›

Use 14-inch Dutch lid
Turn Dutch lid upside down on lid stand
Use 20 hot coals under lid

1 pound fish fillets
1/2 teaspoon onion powder
3/4 teaspoon Season-All
Dash of mace
2 tablespoons soft butter
1 tablespoon lemon juice

1 piece heavy duty aluminum foil

Lay fish fillets on a piece of heavy-duty aluminum foil.
In a small bowl mix together onion powder, Season-All and mace.
  Next mix in butter and lemon juice with spices. Spread this
  mixture over fillets on only one side.

Fold foil over top and seal ends to make a package. You want the
  foil tight enough so juice will not run out.

Place foil package on 14-inch Dutch lid. Cook until fish can be
  flaked with a fork, or about 20 minutes. After about 10 minutes
  of cooking turn package over in order to cook both sides.

Another recipe for cooking the fillets is to use 3/4 teaspoon salt, 1/2
  teaspoon dill weed, 1/8-teaspoon pepper and dash MSG, in place
  of onion salt, Season-All and mace. Cook as in directions above.

Another recipe is use 3/4 teaspoon salt, 1/4 teaspoon crushed rosemary, 1/8 teaspoon tarragon, 1/8 teaspoon crushed fennel seed
  and a dash of pepper in place of onion salt, Season-All and
  mace. Cook as in directions above.

How to make a package with aluminum foil:
Bring both sides of foil together, length wise, and crimp pieces
  together as tight as possible. With a firm hold; start folding
  down towards fish, pressing the foil tight with each turn.
  Continue till foil is flat against fish.
On each end, crimp the first turn as firm as possible. Continue to
  fold and crimp as tight as possible till you reach the fish.

The purpose is to keep the liquid inside package while cooking.

This dinner is quick with no pans to wash. The package allows the
seasonings to saturate the fish with great flavors.

Fried Oysters

Use 12-inch Dutch
Use 15 hot coals on bottom in checkerboard pattern
(No top heat)

1 quart jar oysters
1 egg
2 tablespoons all purpose flour
1 cup cracker crumbs
dash salt
dash pepper
1 lemon
1 cup milk
2 tablespoons salad oil
Fresh parsley for a garnish

Wash oysters well and wipe dry with a paper towel.

Season with salt and pepper.

Mix together egg and milk in a bowl.

Mix flour and breadcrumbs in another bowl.

Dip oysters in egg mixture then roll in flour mixture. They are
now ready to fry.

Pour salad oil into Dutch and set over hot coals. After oil reaches
medium heat, place oysters in Dutch and fry till golden brown.

Serve with lemon juice and garnish with parsley.

The secret here is be sure and wash the oysters well to make sure
all the sand is removed.

Packaged Poached Halibut
with Lemon Sauce

Use lid from 14-inch Dutch
Use 20 hot coals in checkerboard pattern under lid
Turn lid upside down on lid stand
Pre-heat lid

2 1-pound halibut steaks
2 tablespoons melted butter
1 teaspoon tarragon flakes
Juice of 1 lemon
1 teaspoon lemon pepper
1 teaspoon minced garlic

1 piece heavy-duty aluminum foil

Trim skin off halibut. Wash fish thoroughly and dry with paper
    towel.

In a bowl mix together butter, tarragon, lemon juice, lemon pepper
    and garlic.

Lay fish on foil and brush on butter mixture, turn fish over and
    brush remaining butter mixture on fish.

Lay the fish on the foil and follow the instructions in the recipe
    Fish Fillets Cooked in a Package on how to make a package, in
    this section.

Lay package, with **crimped side up,** on pre-heated lid and bake
    for 7 minutes. Turn package over and bake another 7 minutes.

Remove from heat and with a knife cut foil open to serve fish from
    foil. Spoon liquid, from package, over fish.

With this one, there is no pan to wash.

People tend to overcook fish if it is fried or baked. Poaching guar-
    antees the fish to come out moist every time.

Pan Fried Trout

Use 14-inch Dutch lid

Use 20 hot coals in checkerboard pattern under lid
sitting on lid stand ·

Preheat Dutch lid

Clean trout
Dry trout with paper towel

Mix 1 egg to 1/2 cup milk and
whip till smooth

Mix equal parts all purpose flour and cracker crumbs. To this mixture add 1 teaspoon Season All and 1/4 teaspoon onion powder.
Salt and pepper to taste.

Dip fish in milk and roll in flour and crumb mixture.

Pour enough salad oil on lid to fry trout. Fry on one side, turn over
and fry other side.

Serve with melted butter and lemon juice over fish.

This is one of the best ways to use a Dutch lid for cooking. Good
for cooking eggs, fried potatoes, breakfast meats and pancakes.

Poached Salmon in a Package

Use 14-inch Dutch lid
Set Dutch lid on a lid holder with 20 hot coals on bottom

2 pounds salmon fillet
1 cup Minute Maid
   Orange Juice
   Concentrate (**do not
   mix with water)**
4 tablespoons Lea
   and Perrins
   Worchestershire Sauce
Heavy duty
   aluminum foil

Clean Salmon and lay on
   an 18-inch by 24-inch
   piece of foil.

Spread 2 tablespoons worchestershire sauce over flesh
   side of fish.

Pour 1/2 cup of orange juice over fish.

Turn fish over and repeat process.

Fold foil into a package as given in the directions in the recipe
   Fish Fillet Cooked in a Package in this section.

Lay foil package on hot lid with **crimped side up** and cook for 10
   minutes, turn package over and cook another 10 minutes.
   During both cooking times lift package and give it a half turn
   every 5 minutes. The half turn works like the hands of a clock.

Remove from heat, cut foil and serve from foil.

Shrimp Supper

Use 12-inch Dutch
Use 15 hot coals in checkerboard pattern on bottom
(No top heat)

1 pound shrimp
1/4 cup butter
2 tablespoons lemon juice
1/2 teaspoon tarragon leaves
1/2 teaspoon dry mustard
1 teaspoon parsley flakes
1 teaspoon chives
1/8 teaspoon cayenne or red pepper
3/4 teaspoon season-all
1/8 teaspoon garlic powder

Clean, shell and devein shrimp. Melt butter in Dutch then add all
the seasonings and lemon juice.

Sauté shrimp in butter and seasonings about 8 minutes turning
once.

Serve over rice.

Southern Fried Shrimp

Use 10-inch Dutch

Use 10 to 12 hot coals in a checkerboard pattern on bottom
No top heat

2 cups cleaned (shell and devein) shrimp
1/4 cup all purpose flour
1 egg, beaten
2 tablespoons milk
1/2 cup cracker crumbs
1 1/2 teaspoon salt
1/4 teaspoon pepper
5 tablespoons salad oil

Mix flour, cracker crumbs, salt and pepper together.

Mix eggs and milk together.

Dip shrimp in egg mixture and roll in flour mixture.

Pour salad oil in hot Dutch and sauté 3 to 5 minutes until golden
brown.

Serve with lemon juice.

LAMB

Lamb Stew with Dumplings

Use 12-inch Dutch oven

Use 16 coals on lid, in a ring on edge
Use 8 coals on bottom in checkerboard pattern

2 pounds lamb
4 cups cubed potatoes
2 cups quartered carrots
2 cups small peeled and quartered onions
1 cup quartered tomatoes
1/2 teaspoon salt
1/4 teaspoon pepper
1/2 teaspoon paprika
2 tablespoons chopped parsley
1/2 cup all purpose flour

Cut meat in small pieces and roll in flour, salt and pepper.
    Brown in 2 tablespoons salad oil. Cover with hot water
    and simmer 1 1/2 hours. Then add onions, carrots, pota-
    toes, tomatoes and seasonings. Simmer until tender.

Dumplings:
1 cup flour
2 teaspoon baking powder
1/2 teaspoon salt
1/2 cup milk
Sift salt, baking powder and flour together.

Add milk and make soft dough.

Drop with spoon into hot stew and steam covered for
    10 minutes.

Remove from heat and serve with dumplings over stew.

Pork

Baby Back Ribs and Sauerkraut

Use 14-inch Dutch
Use 17 coals on bottom in checkerboard pattern
Bottom heat only

3 pounds baby back ribs cut into serving sizes
1 quart canned sauerkraut
2 cups pearl onions
4 Granny Smith apples peeled and sliced
1 yellow onion quartered
1/2 teaspoon minced garlic
1 pound Hillshire pork sausage cut into slices
2 large white potatoes peeled and cut into cubes

Sear ribs over medium high heat in 14-inch Dutch. Remove ribs
and set aside. Brown sausage in Dutch, remove sausage and set
aside. Remove all remaining fat except about 1 tablespoon.
Sauté onions until clear in color, stirring constantly, add garlic,
ribs, sauerkraut, potatoes, apples and simmer until potatoes
and apples are tender. May need to remove some coals to maintain just a simmer. If mixture is a little dry, add small amount
of water. Last 5 minutes of cooking, add sausage slices.

Cranberry Pork Roast

Use 12-inch Dutch
Use 9 coals on bottom
Use 15 coals on lid in ring
Trivet
Meat thermometer

4 pounds boneless pork loin roast
1 (16 ounce) can whole berry cranberry sauce
1 (1 ounce) package dried onion soup mix
2 tablespoons salad oil
2 cups chicken broth

Heat oil in Dutch, brown roast on all sides. Place trivet under
 roast. Add chicken broth.

Place meat thermometer into thickest part of roast and cook until
 thermometer reaches 155 degrees to 160 degrees.

After first half-hour of roasting, baste roast every 15 minutes with
 cranberry and onion mixture sauce. If any sauce is left over
 after roast is cooked, serve sauce on side.

Sauce
Mix cranberry sauce and onion mix in small Dutch until mixture
 is hot.

Idaho Dutch Quick Dinner

Use 12-inch Dutch
Use 12 to 15 coals on bottom in checkerboard pattern
Bottom heat only

2 tablespoons butter
1/2 cup yellow onion chopped
1/2 cup green bell pepper chopped
1 clove garlic – minced
2 (16 ounce each) cans whole tomatoes cut in pieces
1 teaspoon lemon juice
1/2 teaspoon salt
1/4 teaspoon black pepper
1/4 teaspoon ground thyme leaves
4 Idaho potatoes peeled and sliced thin
1 pound cooked ham cubed

Melt butter over medium heat; add onion, green pepper and garlic,
    cook until tender. Stir in remaining ingredients. Cover, simmer
    30 to 45 minutes or until potatoes are tender.

Italian Dutch Pork Chops

Use 12-inch Dutch
Use 15 coals on bottom in checkerboard
Bottom heat only

4 center cut pork chops about 3/4 inch thick
1 teaspoon vegetable oil
1/4 cup Italian dressing
1/4 cup your favorite barbecue sauce

Heat oil in 12-inch Dutch and brown chops on only one side. Turn
    over pork chops.

Mix barbecue sauce and Italian dressing and pour over chops.
    Cover and simmer for 5 to 8 minutes, or until chops are done
    and tender.

Louisiana Blackened Baby Back Ribs

Use 14-inch Dutch
Use 11 coals on bottom in checkerboard pattern
Use 21 coals in ring on lid
Trivet

3 to 4 pounds baby back
   ribs cut into serving
   size

Sauce
2/3 cup water
3 1/2 tablespoons butter
1 tablespoon plus 1 tea-
   spoon fresh lemon juice
2 tablespoons dry mustard
2 tablespoons plus 2 teaspoons chili powder
2 teaspoons granulated sugar
2 teaspoons paprika
3/4 teaspoon onion powder
3/4 teaspoon garlic powder
1/8 teaspoon cayenne pepper

(Prepare sauce ahead using a baby Dutch or in a small pan on
   regular stove. Sauce may be made ahead and taken on trip.)
Combine all the sauce ingredients in Dutch or sauce pan and simmer 30 minutes.

Place trivet in 14-inch Dutch and set ribs on trivet with meat side
   up. Add 2 cups hot water. Set on coals and cover. Roast about 1-
   1/2 hours. Remove hot coals from bottom and place coals on lid.

Baste both sides of ribs and then continue basting several times
   while cooking for another 15 minutes. Make sure meat side is
   facing up. By putting all the heat on the top, it acts as a broiler.

Pork Sausage and Rice

Use 12-inch Dutch
Use 15 hot coals on bottom in checkerboard pattern
Bottom heat only

1 pound Jimmy Dean regular pork sausage
1 small clove garlic crushed
1 green pepper diced
1 cup onions diced
1 cup celery diced

Mix the above ingredients and fry till sausage and vegetables are
    done. Stirring often.

Remove excess grease from sausage if necessary.

Add:
1 can cream of mushroom soup
1/2 soup can of water
1 can Chicken Noodleo's Soup
Mix well

Add 6 to 8 sliced mushrooms.

Cook for 30 minutes.

Salt and Pepper (if needed) to taste.

Serve over hot rice.

Ranch House Style Barbecued Ribs

Use 12-inch Dutch
Use 10 coals on bottom in checkerboard pattern
Use 19 coals on lid
Trivet

2 pounds baby back ribs cut
    into serving sizes
1 tablespoon paprika
3/4 teaspoon salt
1 1/2 teaspoon onion powder
1 1/2 teaspoon garlic powder
1 teaspoon black pepper
3/4 teaspoon cayenne pepper –
    amount may vary on taste
    preferred
3/4 teaspoon crushed thyme
3/4 teaspoon crushed oregano
2 tablespoons brown sugar
2 cups hot water

Mix well brown sugar and seasonings.

Place trivet in Dutch and place ribs on trivet with meat side up.
    Add hot water and bake for 1 hour. Sprinkle seasoning and
    sugar mixture lightly on bottom side of ribs. Sprinkle heavy on
    meat side of ribs.

At this time remove bottom heat and place bottom coals on lid
    with other hot coals. Bake another 30 minutes.

By putting all the coals on lid, for the last 30 minutes, the top
    heat will work as a broiler.

Sugar Cured Baked Ham with Basting Sauce

Use 14-inch Dutch
Use 9 coals on bottom checkerboard patter
Use 15 coals in a ring on preheated lid
Trivet
Meat thermometer
Line Dutch with foil,
    bringing foil up on sides

Sauce for basting
4 cups pineapple juice
4 cloves of garlic – crushed
1 inch piece fresh ginger
    peeled and sliced in
    small pieces

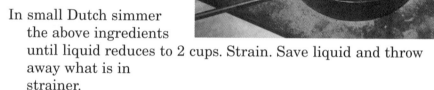

In small Dutch simmer
    the above ingredients
    until liquid reduces to 2 cups. Strain. Save liquid and throw
    away what is in
    strainer.

8 pound ham
16 whole cloves
1/4 teaspoon ground cloves
1/2 cup mustard
1 cup light brown sugar
10 pineapple rings sliced & drained, **save liquid**
10 maraschino cherries
10 wooden toothpicks

Using a sharp pointed knife make 16 small cuts, in uniform pat-
    tern, in ham. Place a whole clove in each cut.
Brush ham with mustard. Sprinkle 1/4 teaspoon ground cloves on
    top. Sprinkle brown sugar and pat into the mustard.
Stick a toothpick into a maraschino and stick toothpick, with cher-
    ry, evenly into the ham.
Place a slice of pineapple over cherry, so cherry will be stuck in
    ham with the pineapple ring around cherry.

Pour the liquid, from pineapple slices, plus 1/4 cup water, into foil
    lined Dutch.
Place meat thermometer into thickest portion of ham.
Place trivet in Dutch and place ham on trivet.
Set Dutch on hot coals and place pre-heated lid on Dutch.
After 1 hour of cooking, baste ham every 20 minutes.
When the thermometer reaches 140 degrees, remove from heat.
If more liquid is needed add hot water.
If any basting sauce is left over, serve at table over ham slices.

Sunday Pork Loin Roast

Use 12-inch Dutch
Use 7 coals on bottom in checkerboard pattern
Use 15 coals in ring on lid
Trivet
Meat thermometer

5 pound boneless pork roast
2 cup hot water
1/2 teaspoon fresh ground black pepper
1/2 teaspoon dry mustard
1/2 teaspoon ground thyme
1/2 teaspoon ginger
10 to 12 whole cloves
1/2 cup honey
1/2 cup orange juice
1/2 teaspoon MSG

Mix together pepper, mustard, thyme, ginger and MSG and rub
    roast. Brown on all sides in Dutch that has been well sprayed
    with a no stick cooking spray. Remove roast and insert a trivet
    in the Dutch. Push the whole cloves, evenly spaced, into the top
    of the roast. Insert thermometer in thickest part of roast. Place
    roast in Dutch and add hot water. Place Dutch on hot coals and
    place pre-heated lid on Dutch. Roast until thermometer reads
    170 degrees, or about 1 1/2 hours.

Basting Sauce
Mix 1/2 cup honey and 1/2 cup concentrated orange juice.

Brush sauce on roast, several times, after the first hour
of cooking.

> **When baking or cooking about every 15
> minutes use a lid lifter, rotate the lid on the
> Dutch oven about a quarter turn. At the same
> time, also turn the entire Dutch about a quar-
> ter of a turn. This will help eliminate hot spots
> on both top and bottom heat.**

Sweet and Sour Pork

Use 12-inch Dutch
Use 9 coals on bottom
Use 15 coals in ring on
 lid with 2 coals in
 middle

2 pounds pork loin cut
 into 3/4-inch cubes
2 tablespoons butter
3/4 pound bean sprouts
1 cup sliced water chest-
 nuts
1 medium red onion
 sliced thin
2 cups sliced celery
6 tablespoons cornstarch
1 (20 ounce) can pineapple chunks **drained – save juice**.
1/2 cup soy sauce
1 tablespoon grated fresh ginger root
1 bunch green onions chopped
1 red bell pepper cubed into 1-inch squares
1 green bell pepper cubed into 1-inch squares
1 cup sliced mushrooms
1 cup apple cider vinegar
1/4 cup water
1 cup ketchup

Mix cornstarch with water, add pineapple juice, soy sauce, vinegar
 and ketchup and set aside. Melt butter in Dutch, add pork and
 cover and cook until almost done, stirring frequently. Add all
 the vegetables except mushrooms and sauté 3 to 5 minutes or
 until cooked crisp tender. Add mushrooms and cook 2 more minutes. Add liquid mixture and stir till meat and vegetables thick-
 en.

Serve over white rice.

Notes

Poultry

Baked Lemon Chicken Breast

Use 12-inch Dutch
Use a trivet
Use 16 coals in a ring on edge of lid
Use 8 coals on bottom in checker board pattern

6 boneless skinless chicken breasts
1 tablespoon cornstarch
Juice from 1 fresh lemon
1 cup water
Fresh milk

Mix the following spices together
1/2 teaspoon paprika
1/2 teaspoon dried minced onions
1/2 teaspoon garlic powder
1/4 teaspoon tarragon
1/4 teaspoon marjoram
1/2 teaspoon poultry seasonings
1/2 teaspoon sweet basil

Salt and pepper to taste

Wash and wipe dry the chicken breasts. Rub spices on both sides
of chicken. Place trivet in Dutch and add 1-cup water. Place
chicken on trivet. Pour the juice from lemon over chicken. Place
lid on Dutch and bake until meat is fork tender, basting several
times while cooking.

When chicken is done, remove chicken and trivet from Dutch.
Place chicken in a warm area. De-glaze bottom of Dutch. (See
terminology.) Mix cornstarch with enough fresh milk to make a
smooth paste. Thicken pan mixture with cornstarch mixture to
make gravy. If there is not enough liquid in Dutch add a little
fresh milk. Pour over chicken before serving.

Cajun Chicken

Use 12-inch Dutch
Use 15 coals in a ring on edge of lid
Use 7 coals on bottom in checker board pattern

3 1/2 pounds frying chicken
    cut into pieces
1/4 cup flour
1/4 cup salad oil
1 cup yellow onion thinly
    sliced
2 cloves of garlic minced
1 green bell pepper cut
    into about 1/2-inch
    square pieces
1/2 cup celery chopped
1 bay leaf
2 cans (13 ounce each) stewed tomatoes
Dash tabasco sauce

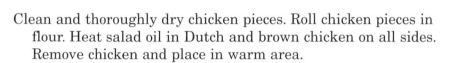

Clean and thoroughly dry chicken pieces. Roll chicken pieces in
    flour. Heat salad oil in Dutch and brown chicken on all sides.
    Remove chicken and place in warm area.

Place onion, garlic, green pepper and celery in Dutch and sauté for
    about 5 minutes.

Cut stewed tomatoes in small pieces, place in Dutch and add
    Tabasco sauce and bay leaf and bring to boil. Add chicken, place
    lid on Dutch and simmer until chicken is fork tender.

Camp Dutch Barbecue Chicken

Use 12-inch Dutch
Use 16 coals on lid in a ring around edge
Use 8 coals on bottom in checkerboard pattern

3 1/2 pounds boneless skinless chicken breasts cut into bite size
   pieces
1/4 cup oil
1 large yellow onion sliced thin
1 medium green bell pepper chopped
1 teaspoon minced garlic
2 cans (10 3/4 ounces each) condensed tomato soup
3 tablespoons brown sugar
3 tablespoons worcestershire sauce
3 tablespoons lemon juice (may use apple cider vinegar)
3 tablespoons prepared mustard
1/4 teaspoon Tabasco sauce
1 teaspoon fresh ginger root grated

Clean and dry chicken. Heat oil in Dutch and sauté chicken until
   chicken turns white. Remove chicken and in remaining oil sauté
   onion, green bell pepper, ginger root and garlic for about 5 minutes.

Add soup, brown sugar, worcestershire sauce, tabasco sauce, mustard and lemon juice. Bring to a boil; add chicken, cover and
   simmer for about 30 minutes, or until chicken is tender. Serve
   over rice.

With this recipe you get the great taste of barbecue chicken without taking your bulky barbecue on that trip camping or fishing.
   This will satisfy the healthy appetites and is really a crowd
   pleaser.

Chicken and Quick Dumplings

Use 12-inch Dutch
Use 16 coals on lid in a ring around edge
Use 8 coals on bottom in checkerboard pattern

3 pound fryer chicken
    cut into 8 pieces
1 tablespoon salad oil
1 1/2 cup Bisquick mix
1 cup water
1/2 cup milk
1 medium yellow onion
    minced
2 carrots minced
1 small can cream of
    chicken soup
1/4 teaspoon sage
1/4 teaspoon garlic
1/4 teaspoon Italian seasonings
Salt and pepper to taste
1/2 cup Bisquick mix

Using 1/2 cup Bisquick, coat chicken pieces. Heat oil in Dutch and
    fry chicken until browned.

In a separate bowl mix soup, onion, garlic, carrots and water. Pour
    over chicken. Cover Dutch and simmer about 30 minutes or
    until chicken is done.

In another bowl, mix 1 1/2 cups Bisquick, sage, Italian seasonings
    and milk together to form a soft dough. Pinch off small pieces of
    dough and drop into simmering chicken. Simmer **uncovered** 7
    to 10 minutes or until dumplings are cooked.

This one pot dinner will bring back memories when moms all over
    America would not be without a box of Bisquick in the kitchen.

Chicken and Spaghetti Sauce

Use 12-inch Dutch
Use 16 coals on lid in a ring around edge
Use 8 coals on bottom in checkerboard pattern

3 to 4 boneless, skinless checked breasts cut into bite size pieces
1 teaspoon minced garlic
1 teaspoon Italian seasonings
1 can (15 ounces) Chef Boyardee Spaghetti Sauce with meat
    (no other kind)
3 tablespoons butter
2 cups celery diced
8 ounces fresh mushrooms cleaned and sliced
1/2 teaspoon pepper
1/2 teaspoon salt

Sprinkle chicken with garlic, Italian Seasoning, salt and pepper.
    Set aside.

Melt butter in Dutch and sauté chicken until color turns white.
    Remove chicken from Dutch. Sauté mushrooms in remaining
    butter for about 5 minutes. Return chicken to Dutch and add
    spaghetti sauce then simmer 10 minutes stirring occasionally.
    Add celery and simmer for 10 minutes. If chicken looks dry, add
    1/4 cup water with the celery.

Use the garlic, salt and pepper to taste. Serve over cooked white
    rice. Serve with garlic French bread.

I found this recipe while waiting in my dentist's office, more than
    35 years ago, reading a magazine. I tried it at home, later made
    a few changes and have been cooking it since that time. It was
    a lucky day for me to have to sit and wait for the dentist.

Chicken and Sweet Pepper Stir Fry

Use 12-inch Dutch
Use 18 coals on lid in ring around edge
Use 11 coals on bottom in checkerboard pattern

2 boneless, skinless chicken breast halves cut into bite
    size pieces
3 tablespoons soy sauce
1 tablespoon dry sherry
2 tablespoons salad oil
1 medium yellow onion cut
    in 8 wedges
1 green bell pepper thinly
    sliced
1 red bell pepper thinly
    sliced
1 1/2 cup fresh mushrooms
    cleaned and sliced
1 teaspoon fresh ginger root
    grated

1 can (8 ounces) bamboo shoots drained
3/4 cup chicken stock
2 tablespoons cornstarch
Salt and pepper to taste

Mix chicken stock, soy sauce, dry sherry and cornstarch together
    and set aside.

Heat 1 tablespoon of oil in Dutch and stir-fry onions till they are
    tender. Add peppers and stir-fry till they are crisp tender. Add
    mushrooms and stir-fry only 1 minute, transfer ingredients to a
    plate and set aside in a warm area. Heat remaining oil in
    Dutch, add ginger root and stir-fry about 15 seconds. Place
    chicken in Dutch and stir-fry till chicken turns white. Return
    vegetables to Dutch, add bamboo shoots, and stir-fry until
    chicken is thoroughly cooked. Pour chicken stock, soy sauce, dry
    sherry and cornstarch mixture over chicken and vegetables and
    stir-fry until sauce thickens. Serve over white rice.

If you feel the sauce is too thick, thin with a little dry sherry.

Chicken and Vegetable Dutch

Use 12-inch Dutch
Use 16 coals on lid in a ring around edge
Use 8 coals in checkerboard pattern on bottom

8 chicken thighs
Salt and pepper to taste
1 tablespoon salad oil
4 red potatoes peeled and sliced
1 medium red onion peeled and thinly sliced
1/2 pound fresh mushrooms cleaned, stemmed and quartered
1 large tomato diced
1/2 cup chicken stock
1/2 cup white wine or dry sherry
1/2 teaspoon dried oregano crush with fingers
1 tablespoon fresh parsley for garnish (optional)
1 tablespoon cornstarch
3 tablespoons cold water

Clean chicken and pat dry. Remove skin and trim off any excess
fat. Sprinkle chicken with salt and pepper.

Heat oil in Dutch and sauté chicken until evenly browned on all
sides. Remove chicken and place in a warm area.

Alternately place the chicken, potatoes, onion, mushrooms and
tomatoes in layers in the Dutch.

In a small bowl blend together the chicken stock and wine (or
sherry). Pour mixture over chicken and vegetables. Sprinkle top
with oregano. Use oregano to taste as with salt and pepper.

Bring to a boil, then simmer about 20 minutes or until chicken is
thoroughly cooked and vegetables are done.

After meal is through cooking, remove 1 1/2 cups liquid juices and
place in small Dutch and bring to boil. Mix 1 tablespoon cornstarch with 3 tablespoons cold water and gently pour into liquid, stirring constantly, until liquid thickens to make a gravy.
Spoon gravy over chicken and vegetables before serving.

Chicken Breasts with Tomatoes

Use 12-inch Dutch
Use 16 coals on lid in a ring around edge
Use 8 coals on bottom in checkerboard pattern

4 to 6 boneless skinless chicken breasts cut into bite size pieces
1/4 teaspoon pepper
1/2 teaspoon salt
3 tablespoons butter
8 ounces sliced mushrooms
1 1/2 cup chicken broth
1 cup frozen peas
1 cup green onions chopped
3/4 cup dry sherry
1/4 cup water
1 tablespoon cornstarch
3 small tomatoes peeled and cut into eighths (1/8th)

Melt butter in Dutch and cook chicken till chicken is white in
    color. Remove chicken. Add onions and mushrooms and sauté.
    Add peas, broth and sherry and return chicken to Dutch.
    Simmer for 20 minutes.

Mix cornstarch and water and constantly stirring, gently pour
    over chicken mixture.

After mixture has thickened, place tomatoes on top, cover and gen-
    tly simmer for 2 minutes.

Serve over rice.

This recipe is just the thing if you have unexpected company and
    you need a great meal in a hurry.

Chicken Cordon Bleu

Use 10-inch Dutch
Use 14 coals on lid in a ring on edge
Use 6 coals on bottom in checkerboard pattern

4 boneless skinless chicken breasts halves
4 slices ham
4 slices Swiss cheese
1/2 cup breadcrumbs
3/4 teaspoon paprika
1/4 cup melted butter
Salt and pepper to taste
Toothpicks
1 can (10-ounce) cream of chicken soup
1 cup milk

Clean and pat dry chicken breasts and flatten till about 1/4 inch
   thick. Place a slice of cheese and ham on each breast and roll
   up each chicken breast, then fasten with toothpicks.

In a bowl, mix breadcrumbs, paprika, salt and pepper together.
   Dip chicken into melted butter, roll in breadcrumbs.

Using salad oil, wipe bottom and sides of Dutch very well. Place
   chicken in Dutch for about 45 minutes.

In separate bowl, mix soup and milk together. For the last 10 minutes of cooking, pour soup mixture over chicken breasts and
   continue baking. Serve with rice.

Chicken Dutch

Use 12-inch Dutch
Use 16 coals on lid in a ring around edge
Use 8 coals on bottom in checkerboard pattern

4 pounds chicken pieces
1/4 cup oil
10 medium fresh mushrooms cleaned and thinly sliced
2 medium yellow onions quartered
2 green bell peppers cleaned and cut into rings
2 teaspoons minced garlic
1 1/2 teaspoons ground sage
2 tablespoons dried rosemary crushed with fingers
1/4 cup sherry or wine
1/2 cup chicken stock
Salt and pepper to taste
1 tablespoon cornstarch

Cut chicken into serving sizes clean and pat dry. Heat oil in Dutch and sauté chicken until golden brown on all sides. Add mushrooms, onions, green peppers, garlic, sage, rosemary mushrooms and chicken stock and continue to cook until the vegetables are tender. Add salt and pepper to taste. Simmer for about 20 minutes longer or until chicken is fork tender and thoroughly cooked. **Do not let Dutch go dry**. If necessary, use more chicken stock. Once cooked, remove and place on a serving dish and set aside in a warm area.

Add 1-tablespoon cornstarch to 1/4 cup sherry or wine and use to thicken 2 cups of juices left in Dutch. Once thickened pour over chicken and serve.

Chicken Greek Style with White Rice

Use 12-inch Dutch
Use 16 coals on lid in a ring around edge
Use 8 coals on bottom in checkerboard pattern

1 medium chicken
1/4 cup oil
1 medium yellow onion chopped
1 can (4 ounces) tomato paste
1/2 teaspoon white granulated sugar
3 tablespoons water
3 cups boiling water
1 cup white rice uncooked
1/4 cup melted butter
Salt and pepper to taste

Cut chicken into serving sizes, clean and pat dry. Heat oil in Dutch
and sauté chicken until brown on all sides. Add onions, tomato
paste, 3 tablespoons water, salt and pepper. Cover and simmer
about 20 minutes or until chicken is thoroughly cooked. Add
boiling hot water to Dutch. Sprinkle rice over chicken and cook
until rice is done and the liquid has been absorbed. Place on a
serving dish and pour butter over top.

Serve with French bread.

Chicken Paprika

Use 12-inch Dutch
Use 16 coals on lid in a ring around edge
Use 8 coals on bottom in checkerboard pattern

4-pound chicken
3 tablespoons oil
1 medium onion thinly sliced
1 teaspoon pepper
1 teaspoon salt
1 teaspoon paprika
2 teaspoons minced garlic
1/2 cup all purpose flour
1 cup chicken stock
12 ounces sour cream

Cut chicken into serving sizes, clean and pat dry. In a bowl, mix
together flour, paprika, salt and pepper.

In Dutch heat oil and sauté onion slices till tender. Coat chicken
with flour mixture then sauté. Add chicken and sauté until
brown. Add chicken stock and garlic. Salt and pepper to taste.
Simmer for 30 minutes or until the chicken is thoroughly
cooked. Add sour cream and simmer about 5 to 10 minutes.
Remove from heat and serve with white rice or noodles.

This is good served over rice or noodles, but for a real treat, serve
it over homemade noodles in the Miscellaneous section.

Chicken Sour Cream Enchiladas by Alma

Use 14-inch Dutch
Use 15 coals on lid in a ring around edge. **Preheat lid**
Use 15 coals on bottom in checkerboard pattern

1 can (12.5 ounces) white chicken meat
1 cup sharp cheddar cheese grated
1 cup Monterey jack cheese grated
12 ounces sour cream
2 bunched green onions sliced using some tops
1/2 cup chopped cilantro
Salt and pepper to taste
Mix the above ingredients together and set aside

1 large can enchilada sauce (either red or green)
8 to 10 corn tortillas
Non stick cooking spray
1/2 teaspoon cooking oil

Heat Dutch. Spray tortilla on each side and quickly fry on each
side until the tortilla is soft. Set them aside.

Heat enchilada sauce with 1/2 teaspoon cooking oil. Heat only till
lukewarm. Dip each tortilla in the sauce and lay flat. Fill with
chicken mixture and roll tortilla. Set aside.

Place in Dutch and pour remaining sauce over them. Sprinkle tops
with both kinds of cheese. Heat until enchiladas are heated
throughout and cheese is melted.

You have to try this to fully understand how delicious it is.

Chicken Stir Fry

Use 12-inch Dutch
Use 18 coals on lid in a ring around edge
Use 11 coals on bottom in checkerboard pattern

3 boneless, skinless chicken breasts halves cut into
    bite size pieces
1/2 cup broccoli florets
1/2 cup snow peas
1/2 cup carrots thinly sliced
1/2 red bell pepper cut into julienne slices
1 envelope onion soup mix (6 ounce package)
1 teaspoon cornstarch blended with 1 tablespoon water
1/2 teaspoon fresh ginger root grated
1 1/2 cups water
2 teaspoons soy sauce
1 teaspoon rice wine vinegar
1 1/3 cups cooked white rice
1 tablespoon salad oil or spray Dutch with non-stick
    cooking spray

Sauté vegetables until they are crisp tender. Remove and set
    aside. Spray or oil Dutch and stir-fry chicken until it turns
    white in color.

Blend cornstarch with 1 1/2 cups water then add soup mix, ginger,
    soy sauce and vinegar and mix till smooth. Stir into chicken,
    add vegetables and cook until chicken is cooked through.
    Remove from heat and serve over rice.

Chicken with Cranberries

Use 12-inch Dutch
Use 16 coals on lid in ring around edge
Use 8 coals on bottom in checkerboard pattern

6 boneless, skinless chicken breast halves
    cut into bite-size pieces
1/3 cup salad oil
3 cloves garlic minced
Salt and pepper to taste
2 green bell peppers cleaned and cut into julienne strips
3 medium yellow onions cleaned and thinly sliced
10 mushrooms cleaned, stemmed and sliced
1/2 cup cider vinegar
1 can (16 ounces) whole cranberry sauce
1 cup orange juice
1 tablespoon cornstarch
2 tablespoons soy sauce

Heat oil in Dutch and cook chicken until pink color turns white. Remove chicken and set aside. Sauté onion, pepper, garlic and mushrooms until crisp tender. Add orange juice, vinegar, chicken and cranberry sauce. Simmer 20 minutes.

Mix 1 tablespoon cornstarch with 2 tablespoons soy sauce and stir in chicken mixture stirring constantly until mixture thickens.

Serve over rice.

Cornish Game Hens

Use 14-inch **deep** Dutch
Use 18 coals on lid in ring around edge
Use 10 coals on bottom in checkerboard pattern
Trivet
Oven thermometer
4 Cornish game hens
1 box Stove Top Stuffing
1/4 to 1/2 teaspoon ground
    sage
1 can (14 1/2 ounces)
    chicken broth
Poultry seasoning
Salt and pepper
Paprika
2 cups hot water
1/4 cup cold water
2 tablespoons cornstarch
Toothpicks

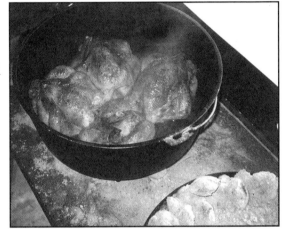

Mix the Stove Top Dressing according to directions on box **except** use chicken broth in place of the water and add 1/4 to 1/2 teaspoon ground sage. Set aside.

Clean Cornish game hens and stuff with dressing. Truss* up hens with string and toothpicks.

Mix poultry seasoning, paprika, salt and pepper, (all to taste) together and sprinkle over chickens.

Place trivet in Dutch and add 2 cups hot water. Place hens on trivet with breast side up. Place oven thermometer in a chicken. Bake until thermometer reaches 190 degrees. Remove hens from Dutch.

De-glaze (see terminology) bottom of Dutch.

Mix 2 tablespoons cornstarch with 1/4 cup cold water and slowly pour into liquid in Dutch to make gravy.

Use a sharp knife to cut the hen in half for a serving. Pour gravy over chicken before serving.

*Truss. At bottom of chicken use toothpicks to hold the chicken together. Using a strong string tie wings together and tie legs together and if necessary also wrap string around toothpicks to help hold the Cornish hen shut. Use only 100 percent cotton string.

This recipe is designed for a great meal and a beautiful presentation in your Dutch oven. It takes a little longer to prepare but your family and friends will truly appreciate your efforts. This is one meal people will talk about with others.

Country Chicken Stew

Use 12-inch Dutch
Use 16 coals on lid in a ring around edge
Use 8 coals on bottom in checkerboard pattern

4 boneless, skinless chicken breast halves cut into
    bite-size pieces
2 tablespoons salad oil
2 cups white onions thinly sliced
3 cups chicken stock
1 cup dry white wine or sherry
2 cans (14 ounces each) stewed tomatoes
2 cups carrots diced
1 cup canned green beans
1/4 cup celery diced
8 small new white potatoes peeled and quartered
1 package (8 ounces) frozen petite peas
1/4 teaspoon dried tarragon crushed with fingers
1/4 teaspoon dried oregano crushed with fingers
1/4 teaspoon dried basil crushed with fingers
2 tablespoons honey
1 tablespoon flour
3 tablespoons milk
1 teaspoon salt
1 teaspoon pepper

Heat oil in Dutch, add chicken and cook until chicken turns white. Add onions to chicken and cook until onions are translucent. Add chicken stock, wine (or sherry), tomatoes, carrots, potatoes, beans and peas. Add honey and all seasonings. Bring to boil then reduce to simmer and cook 35 to 40 minutes, or until vegetables are fork tender.

In a small bowl, mix 1 tablespoon flour with 3 tablespoons milk to make a smooth paste. Slowly stir mixture into the stew; continue stirring constantly, until the stew is slightly thickened. Serve with French bread.

This dinner is what Dutch oven cooking is all about. A complete meal cooked and served from the same pot.

El Paso Chicken

Use 12-inch Dutch
Use 16 coals on lid in a ring around edge
Use 10 coals on bottom in checkerboard pattern

1 medium chicken cut into serving pieces
Salt and pepper to taste
1/2 to 1 cup all-purpose flour
2 tablespoons chili powder
1 teaspoon dried cumin
1/3 cup salad oil
1 cup yellow onion chopped
2 teaspoon garlic minced
1 can stewed tomatoes
3 cups chicken stock hot
1 cup red bell pepper
   chopped
1 cup green bell pepper
   chopped

1 1/2 cups uncooked long grain white rice
1/2 to 1 cup black olives sliced

Clean chicken and pat dry. In a bag, plastic or paper, combine flour, salt and pepper, chili powder and cumin. Mix well. Add a few pieces of chicken at a time to coat chicken with flour mixture.

Heat oil in Dutch. Add chicken and brown chicken on all sides. Remove chicken and place in a warm area. Using the oil remaining in Dutch, sauté the onion and garlic until tender. Add the rice, and cook until rice is lightly browned. Stir often. Add tomatoes, peppers and chicken stock. Stir together. Lay chicken on top of rice mixture and simmer for about 30 to 40 minutes, until rice is cooked. If necessary add more chicken stock.

Serve with the sliced black olives arranged on top of chicken.

When I was a young boy my Uncle Chet cooked this dinner on the South Fork of the Salmon River while on fishing trips. I still can't cook it with out remembering all those great fishing trips. This was probably the only meal he could prepare but I never noticed.

Lemon Chicken Stir-Fry

12-inch Dutch
Use 18 coals on lid in ring around edge
Use 11 coals on bottom in checkerboard pattern

4 boneless, skinless chicken breast halves cut in bite size pieces
2 teaspoons cornstarch
1 teaspoon sugar
1 tablespoon lemon juice
1/2 cup chicken stock
2 tablespoons sherry
2 tablespoons soy sauce
1/4 cup salad oil
Salt and pepper to taste
8 green onions sliced
1 red bell pepper cut in small strips

1 can (4 ounces) sliced mushrooms (drained) – may substitute with
  fresh mushrooms
1 tablespoon grated lemon peel

In a bowl mix together sugar, lemon juice, chicken stock, sherry,
  soy sauce and cornstarch until you have a smooth mixture.

Heat oil in Dutch and cook chicken till white in color. Add salt and
  pepper, remove chicken from Dutch and set in warm area.

In Dutch stir-fry onions, peppers and mushrooms about 1 minute,
  stirring constantly. Add cornstarch mixture and stir-fry about 1
  minute or until vegetables start to thicken.

Return chicken to Dutch, add grated lemon peel and stir-fry till
  chicken is thoroughly cooked.

Serve with rice.

Mexican Chicken by Alma

Use 12-inch Dutch
Use 16 coals on lid in ring about edge
Use 8 coals on bottom in checkerboard pattern
2 1/2 pounds skinless, boneless chicken breasts cut into bite size
  pieces
1 tablespoon oil
1 medium onion chopped
2 teaspoons cumino powder
2 teaspoons black pepper
2 teaspoons salt
1 tablespoon chives chopped
1 tablespoon minced garlic
1 cup S & W stewed tomatoes, original recipe – blend in blender
1 1/2 cups red bell peppers cut into about 1-inch square pieces
1 1/2 cups green bell peppers cut into about 1-inch square pieces
3 cups **hot** water

2 jalapeno peppers

Heat oil in Dutch and add chicken. Simmer, stirring constantly until the chicken is white in color.

Add onion, red and green peppers, tomatoes, chives, garlic, cumino, salt, pepper and **hot water**. Stir gently.

Wash Jalapeno peppers, seed and cut in half, length ways. Add to the chicken mixture. Put on lid and simmer for 30 minutes.

Mix 3 tablespoons cornstarch with 1/2 cup cold water.
After chicken has simmered 30 minutes, **slowly** add cornstarch mixture, stirring constantly, until you reach the desired consistency.

You may not use all the cornstarch mixture.

Warning on the jalapeno peppers:
Once you add the peppers to the chicken mixture taste test often, at least every 5 minutes, to make sure you have the taste you desire. Once you have the taste you want, **remove all the Jalapeno peppers**. Remember the longer the peppers are in the chicken mixture, the hotter your dish will be.

Served with Mexican rice in the Vegetable section and the corn tortillas in the Bread section, you'll think you're in Mexico.

Roasted Chicken

Use 12-inch Dutch
Use 17 coals on lid in a ring around edge
Use 9 coals on bottom in checkerboard pattern
Trivet
Meat thermometer

1 whole chicken (about 3 pounds)
Pinch of sage
Pinch of Italian seasoning
1 teaspoon dried rosemary crushed with your fingers
3 tablespoons melted butter
1 medium onion peeled and quartered
3 potatoes peeled and quartered

2 cups baby carrots
2 cups chicken stock
Salt and pepper to taste

Clean chicken and place on trivet in your Dutch. Brush chicken
with melted butter. Place meat thermometer in thickest part of
chicken. Add chicken stock. Arrange potatoes, onion and carrots
around chicken.

Mix together sage, Italian seasoning, rosemary, salt and pepper
and sprinkle over chicken and vegetables.

Bake till thermometer reaches 190 degrees.

Mom's Old Fashion Chicken and Dumplings

Use 12-inch **deep** Dutch
Use 17 coals on lid in ring around edge
Use 9 coals on bottom in checkerboard pattern

1 three pound whole frying chicken
1 large onion minced
1 large stalk celery minced
3 carrots minced
Salt and pepper to taste

Cut chicken in half. Clean chicken and put into Dutch. Add onion,
celery, carrots, salt and pepper to chicken. Add enough water to
cover entire chicken. Bring to boil and simmer, with lid on
Dutch, for full 30 minutes.

Remove from heat. Place chicken, vegetables and liquid in another
container, with a lid and keep in refrigerator, or an ice chest,
until next day. The next day, remove skin and all bones from
the chicken and discard. Cut the chicken in serving size por-
tions. Place the chicken in the Dutch and add enough of the liquid to cover the chicken plus 1-inch. Heat to a simmer.

Drop dumplings into chicken mixture and simmer 5 to 7 minutes,
or until done.

Ready to serve.

Dumplings
1/2 cup all purpose flour
1 tablespoons melted butter
1 large egg yolk
1/3 cup milk
Pinch of salt

Blend flour, butter, yolk, milk and salt until mixture holds together. Pinch off dough about the size of a walnut and form it into a ball. Drop into the chicken stock and simmer **uncovered** 5 to 7 minutes or until cooked through.

In place of dumplings, the chicken may be served over egg noodles.

The directions for removing chicken from the bone can be used anytime you need chicken meat for such dishes as enchiladas or chicken soup. After I remove the chicken I replace the bones and skin in the broth and boil about 30 minutes. I remove the bones and skin, strain the broth and freeze it for use at a later time. It is cheaper than canned broth and tastes much better.

Pan Fried Chicken

Use 12-inch Dutch
Use 18 coals on bottom in checkerboard pattern
Bottom heat only

1 frying chicken
1/2 cup salad oil
1/2 cup flour
1/2 cup bread crumbs
Salt and pepper to taste

Cut chicken into serving pieces. Clean and pat dry. In a bag, mix
flour, breadcrumbs, salt and pepper together and coat chicken.
Heat oil in Dutch and fry chicken on all sides golden brown.

Oriental Ginger Chicken Stir-Fry

Use 12-inch Dutch
Use 18 coals on lid in a ring around edge
Use 11 coals on bottom in checkerboard pattern

4 boneless, skinless chicken breast halves cut into bite-size pieces
1/4 cup rice wine
1/4 cup soy sauce
2 tablespoons salad oil
1 medium yellow onion cut into 8 wedges
1/2 teaspoon fresh ginger root grated
1/3 cup white wine or sherry
1 package (1pound) frozen mixed vegetables
1 tablespoons cornstarch
1 tablespoon cold water
Salt and pepper to taste

In a bowl mix together the soy sauce and rice wine. Add the chicken and stir to coat the chicken. Cover and let stand at least 10 minutes.

Heat oil in Dutch. Drain chicken **saving the liquid** and stir-fry the chicken and onion until chicken turns white in color.

Add vegetables, ginger root and white wine and cook 4 to 5 minutes or until vegetables are tender crisp. If more liquid is necessary add the soy sauce and rice wine mixture.

Blend 1 tablespoon cornstarch with 1 tablespoon cold water until a smooth texture. Add cornstarch mixture, stirring constantly, until chicken and vegetables mixture is thickened.

Salt and pepper to taste. Serve over rice.

After food is served, if desired, add more soy sauce.

Roasted turkey, candied yams, sage dressing, biscuits.

Roasted Turkey

Use 14-inch Dutch
Use 17 coals in lid in ring around the edge
Use 9 coals on bottom in checkerboard pattern
Meat thermometer
Trivet

1/2 of a 14-pound turkey
2 tablespoons salad oil
1 1/2 teaspoon pepper
3 cups chicken stock

Cut turkey down middle to make 2 equal halves. Place one half of
turkey on trivet with breast side up. Brush oil on turkey and
sprinkle with pepper. Place over thermometer in thickest part
of turkey. Pour chicken stock around turkey. When thermometer
reaches 190 degrees, turkey is done. Do not put coals on the lid
directly over the wing, as this will cause the wing to burn. You
might tie a sting around the turkey wing to hold the wing
down. Remove string before serving.

Shanghai Stir-Fry

Use 12-inch Dutch
Use 18 coals on lid in ring around edge
Use 11 coals on bottom in checkerboard pattern

Non-stick cooking spray
1 cup broccoli florets
1 cup red bell pepper cut into 1 inch cubes
1/2 cup carrots thinly sliced
1 cup green onions sliced using some of the tops
2 tablespoons soy sauce
1/3 cup chicken stock
1 teaspoon minced garlic
1 teaspoon fresh gingerroot grated
1 can (10 3/4 ounces) cream of chicken soup
1 1/2 pounds boneless, skinless chicken breasts cut into bite size
    pieces
Salt and pepper to taste

Mix together chicken stock and soup. Set aside.

Spray inside Dutch with non-stick cooking spray. Stir-fry the broccoli, peppers, carrots and green onions until they are crisp tender. Remove vegetables and put in a holding dish in a warm area and set aside.

Spray Dutch again and stir-fry the chicken until it turns white in color. Add garlic, soy sauce, ginger root and soup mixture. Return vegetables to Dutch, add salt and pepper to taste, and cook until everything is hot.

Serve over hot white long grain rice.

This recipe came home with me from Vietnam where I was working for the Air Force. My wife later added the can of soup to make it creamier. Every time I prepare this dish it brings back memories.

Simmered Chicken Chinese Style

Use 12-inch Dutch
Use 16 coals on lid in ring around edge
Use 8 coals on bottom in checkerboard pattern

1 whole chicken cut into serving pieces
1 tablespoon salad oil
1/3 cup soy sauce
1/3 cup brown sugar
1 tablespoon ketchup
1/2 cup water
1/4 cup dry sherry
1/2 teaspoon red pepper (cayenne) crushed (optional)
1 teaspoon minced garlic
1 bunch green onions sliced with some tops
2 tablespoons cornstarch
1 tablespoon water
2 teaspoons **toasted** sesame seeds

Heat oil in Dutch and brown chicken on all sides.

Mix together soy sauce, 1/2 cup water, ketchup sherry and brown
sugar. Add red pepper, garlic and green onions. Pour over chick-
en, cover and simmer about 45 minutes, turning chicken often.

Remove chicken and place on plate and set in warm area. Save as
much liquid as possible.

Mix 2 tablespoons cornstarch with 1 tablespoon cold water and
stir into the liquid in Dutch stirring constantly until liquid is
thickened.

Spoon liquid over chicken and sprinkle sesame seeds over chicken
before serving.

Spanish Chicken Pot

Use 12-inch Dutch
Use 17 coals on lid in a ring around edge
Use 9 coals on bottom in checkerboard pattern

4 pound fryer chicken cut into serving pieces
2 tablespoon salad oil
1 green bell pepper cut into 1-inch squares
1 red bell pepper cut into 1-inch squares
1 teaspoon cumin powder
1 teaspoon marjoram
1/4 teaspoon cayenne
2 yellow onions cut into wedges
2 cups fresh mushrooms sliced
2 medium tomatoes diced
1/2 cup chicken stock
1/4 cup rice wine vinegar
2 cups ham diced
1/4 cup tomato paste
1/2 cup black olives sliced
1/2 teaspoon minced garlic

Heat oil in Dutch, add chicken and fry until brown on all sides.
Remove chicken and set aside in a warm area. Add peppers,
onions, ham and mushrooms. Cook until crisp tender.

Add chicken stock, vinegar, garlic, marjoram, cumin, cayenne,
tomato paste and tomatoes. Add chicken and simmer until
chicken is done. Sprinkle with black olives.

Marinades and rubs

Barbecue Salt

1 pound brown sugar
1 tablespoon salt
1 tablespoon paprika
2 tablespoons black pepper
1/2 teaspoon cinnamon
1 tablespoon garlic powder
1/2 teaspoon liquid smoke (optional)

This goes well sprinkled on pork, chicken or steak.

Englehorn's Marinade for Steelhead or Salmon

1/2 cup Mazola oil
6 tablespoons soy sauce
1 tablespoon garlic powder
1 teaspoon salt
1/4 teaspoon pepper
1/4 to 1/2 cup rye whiskey
2 tablespoons granulated sugar

Mix the above well and set in refrigerator over night.

When ready to use, marinate fish 2 to 6 hours with flesh side down.

This marinade works well with poached salmon or salmon baked in a package. For directions see *Fish Fillets Cooked in a Package* in the fish section.

Use a 14-inch Dutch lid, place upside down on the lid stand, with 20 hot coals under Dutch lid. Cook 10 to 15 minutes per side. If the fish is 2 inches thick, bake 15 minutes per side. Then enjoy.

Mason Dixon Barbecue Rub

2 tablespoons salt
2 tablespoons sugar
2 tablespoons brown sugar
2 tablespoons cumin powder
2 tablespoons chili powder
2 tablespoons black pepper
1 tablespoon cayenne pepper (red pepper)
4 tablespoons paprika
Mix all the above together and rub on chicken, pork ribs or steak.
Use a salt shaker for even coating. Makes 1 cup.

Mexican Grill Rub for Beef

2 tablespoons chili powder
4 teaspoons garlic salt
2 1/2 teaspoons onion powder
2 teaspoons ground cumin
1 1/2 teaspoon crushed oregano
3/4 teaspoon cayenne pepper (red pepper)

Blend together well. Use about 1/2 teaspoon of rub to each side of
steak. Use a salt shaker for even coating.

Rub for Beef Roast

3 tablespoons paprika
2 tablespoons black pepper
2 tablespoons garlic powder
2 tablespoons dried parsley
2 tablespoons cumin
1 tablespoon thyme
1 teaspoon nutmeg
1 teaspoon onion powder
1 teaspoon chili powder
1 teaspoon ground oregano

Mix well all the above. Use a salt shaker for even coating. This goes well with a beef roast, which is roasted, dry.

Spices and Garlic Marinade

1/4 cup apple cider vinegar
1/4 cup olive oil
1/2 cup Worcestershire Sauce
2 tablespoons fresh minced garlic
1/4 teaspoon salt
1/8 cup finely chopped fresh basil
1/8 cup finely chopped fresh oregano leaves

Mix well all the ingredients. Marinate your steaks for a few hours, in refrigerator, turning occasionally. You may continue to brush your steaks with the marinade while cooking.

Sweet and Sour Marinade

1/2 cup worcestershire sauce
3 tablespoons brown sugar
3 tablespoons olive oil
3 tablespoons Balsamic Vinegar
1/4 teaspoon salt
1 teaspoon fresh minced garlic

Mix all ingredients together. Marinate steaks, in refrigerator, occasionally turning, for a few hours. As steaks are cooking you may continue basting with unused marinade.

Texas Dutch Rub for Pork, Chicken or Beef

1 teaspoon chili powder
1 teaspoon cumin powder
1 teaspoon ground oregano
1 teaspoon garlic salt
1 teaspoon ground thyme
1 teaspoon paprika
1 teaspoon black pepper
1 teaspoon onion powder
Liquid smoke (optional)

Blend together well then add a drop or two of liquid smoke if desired.

Use a salt shaker for even coating.

Notes

Miscellaneous recipes

Baked Apples

Old Dutch Style

Use 10-inch Dutch
Use 5 hot coals in checkerboard pattern on bottom
Use 12 hot coals on lid around edge

4 apples
8 tablespoons brown sugar (may use white granulated sugar)
8 teaspoons butter
1 cup water
Cinnamon or nutmeg

Peel and core apples then cut apples in half. Lay apples on bottom
of Dutch with skin side down. Add 1-tablespoon sugar in center
of each half apple. Place 1-teaspoon butter on top of sugar.

Add 1 cup water on bottom of Dutch.

If desired, add a dash of cinnamon or nutmeg on top of apple.
When apples are tender, remove from heat and serve.

Basting Sauce for Ham

4 cups pineapple juice
4 cloves of garlic, crushed
1 inch piece of fresh ginger root peeled and sliced
1/4 cup light brown sugar

Simmer the above ingredients together until liquid reduces to 2
cups. Strain and keep only the liquid. Cool.

Baste ham after cooking 1 hour. Continue basting every 20 minutes until ham is done.

Batter for Deep Frying Fish or Pork

Mix together
2/3 cup all purpose flour
1/3 cup corn starch
Salt and pepper to taste
1/4 teaspoon garlic powder
1 teaspoon sugar

Add egg and mix well. Add milk to desired texture.

Dip fish or pork for deep-frying.

Breakfast Cooked on a Dutch Lid

Turn a 14-inch camp Dutch lid upside down over a Dutch lid holder. If you have no lid holder, you can use rocks, bricks or whatever you have available to hold the Dutch lid level with 10 to 12 hot coals under the lid. You use the lid as a skillet and you are
ready to cook ham, bacon or sausage, hash brown potatoes and eggs. Also try pancakes and French toast. Any of these items will cook on your lid.

It is also great for cooking fried potatoes, or grilled steaks or any kind of fried meat.

If you're fishing, try cooking your fish in a package. The direction on how to do this is found in the fish section under **Fish fillet cooked in a package**.

Buttermilk Pancakes

Use 14-inch Dutch lid
Set 14-inch lid upside down on lid stand with 10 to 15 hot coals underneath lid

1 1/4 cups all-purpose flour
1 egg
1 1/4 cups buttermilk
1/4 cup granulated sugar
1 heaping teaspoon baking powder
1 teaspoon baking soda
1/4 cup salad oil
Pinch of salt

Measure all dry ingredients into a bowl and blend together.

Add egg and 1/3 of the buttermilk and salad oil then stir. Add remaining buttermilk slowly and a small amount at a time to insure no lumps.

Don't forget. You can fry your breakfast eggs at the same time you're cooking your pancakes. All you need for a good morning is hot syrup and butter.

Chicken, Pepper and Onion Potato Topper

Use 12-inch Dutch
Use 12 to 15 hot coals in checkerboard pattern on bottom
(No top heat)

2 tablespoons butter
1 pound boneless skinless chicken breasts cut into 1-inch square
    pieces
1 medium green or red bell pepper cut into 1-inch square pieces
1 small onion minced
1 teaspoon dried sweet basil leaves
1 (10 3/4 ounce) can cream of chicken soup
1/4 cup water
4 hot baked potatoes **split**

Heat 1 tablespoon butter in Dutch and add chicken. Stir frequently until chicken turns white. Remove chicken from Dutch. Heat 1 tablespoon butter in Dutch, add pepper, onion and basil and cook until pepper and onion are tender crisp.

Add soup and water and heat to a boil.
Add chicken, cover and simmer for about 5 minutes.
Serve over baked potatoes.

This is also delicious served over baking powder biscuits.

Chocolate Sauce

Use 8-inch Dutch oven
6 hot coals on bottom

4 squares semi sweet chocolate squares chopped fine
2 cups hot water
2 tablespoons cornstarch
2 tablespoons cold water
1 1/2 cups granulated sugar
1 tablespoon light corn syrup
Pinch of salt
1 1/2 teaspoons vanilla
1 tablespoon butter

Mix 2 tablespoons cold water with 2 tablespoons cornstarch.

Bring 2 cups of water to a boil.

Add chopped chocolate squares and stir till melted.

Add sugar, syrup and salt.

Add cornstarch mixture and stir till thickens.

Quickly remove from heat and add butter and vanilla.

Makes about 2 1/2 cups.

Serve over Black Forest Cake or anything which calls for a chocolate sauce.

Cranberry Salad

1 pound whole fresh cranberries
3 medium size Delicious apples, peel and remove core
2 medium oranges peeled
3 1/2 cups granulated sugar
3/4 of a 10-ounce package of miniature marshmallows
1/2 pint of **heavy** whipping cream

Grind cranberries, apples and oranges together. Save the juice.
Add 2 1/2 cups sugar and the juice to mixture. Let set **at least**
24 hours in refrigerator.

One hour before you serve the salad whip the whipping cream and
set aside. Add marshmallows to the fruit mixture. Gently fold
in whipping cream and refrigerate till served.

This is an excellent salad served with turkey.

Cranberry Salsa

Use 10-inch Dutch
Use 10 hot coals in checkerboard pattern on bottom
(No top heat)

1 (16 ounce) can whole cranberry sauce
1 red bell pepper diced
1 green bell pepper diced
1 small Jalapeno diced; remove seeds
1/2 cup orange juice
1/2 teaspoon salad oil

In a 10-inch Dutch heat oil, add red pepper, green pepper and
jalapeno pepper. Sauté until peppers start to darken. Remove
Dutch from heat and add cranberries and orange juice. Mix
well. Serve warm over roast beef.

Cranberry Sauce

Use 8-inch Dutch
Use 9 hot coals in checkerboard pattern on bottom
(No top heat)

1/2 cup jellied cranberry sauce
1 (16 ounce) can whole cranberry sauce
1 teaspoon cinnamon
1 teaspoon nutmeg
1 cup diced apples
1 tablespoon lemon juice

Mix everything together in Dutch and set on hot coals. Gently stir
   ingredients together.

Be careful as to not break up the cranberries. Heat until everything is blended well together. The sauce may be served warm
   or cold. It is good with turkey, ham or chicken.

Dumplings

2 cups Bisquick
2/3 cup milk

Mix Bisquick and milk together. Spoon out batter about tablespoon
   size and drop into hot boiling beef stew. Cook uncovered 10 minutes. Cover and cook another 10 minutes.

This recipe also works well with stewed chicken.

Egg Wash

1 egg
1/4 cup cold water

Whip the egg well. Add water and whip together.

This is used to brush on tops of pastry such as cinnamon rolls before baking.

Brush on top piecrust before baking to give the pie a golden color.

When making a 2-crust pie, before top crust is put on pie, brush the edge of the crust with egg wash. When you lay the top crust on the pie, pinch edge of crust and you will get a better seal. This helps prevent any fruit from boiling out the side of the pie.

To get a shine on your French bread or French rolls, brush the top with egg wash before baking.

Homemade Noodles

The kind grandma made.

1 cup all purpose flour
2 tablespoons milk
1/2 teaspoon salt
1 egg beaten

Mix well all the ingredients. Pour out onto a floured surface. With a rolling pin, roll out thin.

Let stand 20 minutes. Roll up the dough. Slice the dough about 1/8 inch thick. Spread noodles out flat to dry, for about 2 hours. Drop into boiling soup or boiling chicken broth and cook 10 minutes, uncovered.

Honey Spice Glaze for Turkey

1/8 teaspoon red pepper (cayenne)
1/4 teaspoon cumin
1/4 teaspoon allspice
1/4 teaspoon salt
1/2 teaspoon garlic powder
1 teaspoon water
2 tablespoons honey

Mix well all the above.

When roasting a turkey, glaze the last 45 minutes of cooking time.

Icing for Cinnamon Rolls

2 cups powdered sugar
Pinch of salt
1/4 teaspoon pure vanilla
1 tablespoon corn syrup
1 tablespoon soft butter

Mix together and add just enough water to make icing thin
    enough to drizzle over rolls.

Let rolls cool before icing them.

Sage Dressing (Stuffing) for Turkey or Chicken

Old Dutch Style

Use 8-inch Dutch
Use 11 hot coals on edge of lid
Use 3 hot coals on bottom

9 cups of diced dried bread
1/3 cup finely chopped onions
1/3 cup raisins, soaked in water
1/3 cup diced apples
2 level tablespoons ground sage
Salt and pepper to taste
3 1/4 cups hot turkey broth

Mix all the dry ingredients together. Pour broth over dry
    ingredients and mix together.

Blend only enough to absorb liquid.

Bake about 30 to 45 minutes or until done.

Notes

Soups and chowders

Aunt Carole's Potato Soup

Use 12-inch Dutch
Use15 hot coals on bottom
No top heat

2 tablespoons cornstarch
2 cups milk
4 tablespoons butter
2 cups water
Salt and pepper to taste
5 to 6 medium boiled potatoes peeled and cubed
8 to 10 sliced bacon, cooked crisp and crumbled
3/4 cup Velveeta

Mix milk and cornstarch until smooth. Add salt and pepper to
taste. Heat, stirring constantly and simmer for 1 minute. Add 2
cups water and return to boil. After a boil add cubed potatoes
and bacon. Add cheese; stir constantly until cheese is melted.

Forty Niner Fish Chowder

Use 12-inch Dutch
Use 15 coals hot coals on bottom
(No top heat)

1 10-ounce package frozen lima beans
2 cups chicken broth
1 (16 ounce) can cream style corn
3 (6 1/2 ounce) cans of chopped clams, **do not drain**
1/2 cup half and half
1/8 teaspoon white pepper
Salt to taste

Cook lima beans in chicken broth till tender. Add corn, clams, half
and half and pepper. Simmer for 3 minutes.

Add salt to taste.

This chowder is quick and easy and will go great on a winter cook-
out.

Mexican Bean Soup

Use 12-inch Dutch
Use 16 hot coals on edge of lid
Use 8 hot coals in checkerboard pattern on bottom

1 onion chopped
1 green bell pepper chopped
1 teaspoon minced garlic
2 1/2 cups vegetable broth
1 (15 ounce) can stewed tomatoes (any type you like, Mexican
    makes it snappier)
1 (15 ounce) can garbanzo beans, **do not drain**
1 (15 ounce) can red beans, **do not drain**
1 (15 ounce) can vegetarian refried beans
1 (15 ounce) can whole kernel corn, **do not drain**
1/2 teaspoon cumin powder

Put all ingredients in a large pot and simmer about 15 minutes.

Clean 2 jalapeno peppers. Washed, cut each into halves. Remove
    seeds.

Add peppers and cook till hot enough to taste, **remove all four
    pieces**.

Continue to cook until you have cooked a total of about 45 min-
    utes.

Makes a good one-dish meal served with corn bread.

If you're on a camping trip, make sure you have a good can opener
    with you and a hardy appetite.

Mexican Vegetable Soup

Use 12-inch Dutch
Use 15 hot coals on bottom
(No top heat)

1 whole chicken
Cover chicken with hot water and boil for 30 minutes. Remove
   from heat and refrigerate over night. Next day, remove skin and
   bones and discard. Cut meat into medium size pieces. Strain
   and save all the chicken stock.

4 potatoes (white or red) cut into chunks, **do not peel**
8 ounces baby carrots
3 stalks celery cut into 1-inch pieces
1 medium sliced zucchini
1 teaspoon minced garlic
1/4 teaspoon cumin powder
Salt and pepper to taste
1/4 cup tomato sauce
1/3 head green cabbage, cut into 4 pieces
1 jalapeno pepper, clean, cut in half and remove seeds

Put all the vegetables and meat into a 12-inch Dutch. Use enough
   chicken stock to completely cover vegetables and meat with at
   least 1 inch liquid over top. Simmer until vegetables are almost
   done, then add cabbage and jalapeno pepper.

After a few minutes, taste to see if soup is hot enough. If so,
   remove jalapeno.

This is the easiest and fastest method for removing chicken from
   the bone and retaining the delicious chicken stock. If there is
   extra chicken stock, freeze it to use later. You'll be glad you did.

Red Chicken and Rice Soup

Use 12-inch Dutch
Use 15 hot coals on bottom in checkerboard pattern
No top heat

1 large onion, chopped
1 large clove of garlic crushed
1 tablespoon butter
2 cups cooked chicken diced
1 teaspoon dijon mustard
4 cups chicken broth
1/2 cup cooked rice
1 1/2 cup ketchup
Salt and pepper to taste

In Dutch melt the butter. Add onion and garlic. Cook, stirring constantly, until onions are done. Add ketchup and mustard. Stir. Add chicken broth and bring to boil. Add chicken meat and rice. Bring to boil. Add salt and pepper to taste. Simmer 5 minutes.

Simple Chicken Vegetable Soup

Use 12-inch Dutch
Use 15 hot coals on bottom
No top heat

2 boneless skinless chicken breast
5 cups water
1/2 medium size onion, finely chopped
2 large carrots cut into size of matchsticks
2 teaspoons chicken paste or 2 cubes of chicken bouillon
1 (14 ounce) can stewed tomatoes, chopped fine
1 tablespoon sweet basil
1 tablespoon dried parsley flakes
1/8 teaspoon garlic powder
1/4 teaspoon poultry seasoning
1 cup cooked rice
Salt and pepper to taste

In Dutch bring to boil, water, whole chicken pieces, chicken paste,
   onion, tomatoes, carrots, garlic, poultry seasoning, parsley
   flakes, basil, salt and pepper. Simmer 25 minutes. Remove
   chicken and cut into small pieces. Return chicken to pot, add
   rice and simmer 5 minutes. Ready to serve.

Spanish Chicken Soup

Use 12-inch Dutch
Use 15 hot coals on bottom
No top heat

3 pounds skinless, boneless chicken breasts cut into
    bite-size pieces
2 tablespoons salad oil
2 large onions, sliced
2 large cloves of garlic, crushed
1 cup water
1 tablespoon brown sugar
1 cup dry white wine
1 tablespoon chopped fresh thyme
1 (16 ounce) can stewed tomatoes
1 1/2 cups chicken broth
1 green pepper cut into strips size of matchsticks

Heat oil in 12-inch Dutch. Add chicken and cook till all sides are
    brown. Remove chicken from Dutch and set aside.

Add onions and garlic to remaining oil in Dutch and cook until
    onions are tender. Return chicken to Dutch and add water,
    sugar, wine, thyme, tomatoes and bell peppers. Simmer, covered,
    for about 40 minutes, until bell peppers are tender.

Serve with French bread.

I really enjoy a bowl of hot delicious soup, especially on
    cold winter days.

South of the Border Ox Tail Soup by Imelda

Use 12-inch Dutch
Use 14 to 15 hot coals on bottom
No top heat

16 pieces ox tail
2 tablespoons salt
1 teaspoon pepper
1 tablespoon minced garlic
1 teaspoon cumin powder
1 large onion cut into eighths

Put ox tail, salt, pepper, garlic, cumin and onion into a 12-inch
Dutch. Add enough water to cover well. Simmer till meat falls
off bone. Additional water will be required to make sure meat is
covered at all times.

Remove bones from meat and return meat to liquid in Dutch.

Add to Dutch
1 pound baby carrots
4 red potatoes, quartered **do not peel**
1/2 head of cabbage quartered
4 small frozen ears of corn

(1 jalapeno pepper)

Simmer till vegetables are tender. Just before vegetables are ready,
add a Jalapeno pepper, which has been cleaned, cut in half with
seeds removed. After soup reaches desired taste, remove both
pieces of pepper.

After spooning soup into bowl squeeze fresh lemon juice over soup.
This is a must.

Served with a corn tortilla this is a meal to surpass any appetite.
This is authentic Mexican style cooking.

Split Pea Soup

Use 12-inch Dutch
Use 15 hot coals on bottom
No top heat

2 cups dry split peas
1 ham bone
3 stalks celery finely chopped
3 carrots finely chopped
1 large onion minced
1/2 teaspoon parsley flakes
Salt and pepper to taste

Put all ingredients into Dutch, cover with water and simmer until
  peas are tender.

Tomato Soup

Use 12-inch Dutch
Use 15 hot coals on bottom
No top heat

2 (14 1/2 ounce each) cans diced tomatoes **do not drain**
2 (10 ounce each) cans condensed tomato soup
1 1/2 cups milk
1 teaspoon sugar
1/2 to 1 teaspoon sweet basil
1/2 to 1 teaspoon paprika
1/8 to 1/4 teaspoon garlic powder
1 8-ounce package cream cheese
1 medium onion, chopped
2 tablespoons butter

Sauté onion in butter until tender, add tomatoes, soup, milk, sugar,
  basil, paprika, and garlic powder. Bring to a simmer and simmer for 10 minutes. Stir in cream cheese until it is melted.

Serve immediately.

Witzig's Old German Clam Chowder

Use 12-inch Dutch
Use 15 hot coals on bottom
No top heat

1 cup yellow onions finely chopped
1 cup celery finely chopped
2 cups finely diced peeled white potatoes
2 (6 1/2 ounce each) cans minced clams **drained** (save liquid)
Salt and pepper to taste

Put vegetables in Dutch. Add salt and pepper. Pour juice from
clams over vegetables and add enough water to barely cover
and simmer until vegetables are barely tender. Remove vegetables and liquid from Dutch.

3/4 cup butter
3/4 cup flour
1 quart half and half
2 tablespoons red wine vinegar

In Dutch melt butter. Add flour and stir constantly. Add half and
half stirring constantly and mix till mixture is smooth and
somewhat thick.

Add vegetables, clams and vinegar. Heat thoroughly.

This is, without a doubt, the best clam chowder you'll ever eat. All
my family loves it, including my fussy eating grandchildren. Try
it and you'll agree.

Vegetables

Chicken Fried Rice

Use 12-inch Dutch
Use 16 coals under Dutch in checkerboard pattern
Bottom heat only

2 boneless skinless chicken breasts
3 green onions chopped using part of the tops
3 tablespoons soy sauce
3 to 4 cups cold white rice cooked
1 egg whipped
1 medium carrot cut into Julienne strips then minced
2 tablespoons salad oil

Cut chicken into small bite-size pieces.

Heat oil in 12-inch Dutch using medium high heat. Fry, stirring constantly, chicken until it loses the pink color and it turns white in color. Add onions and carrots and stir-fry until crisp tender. Add soy sauce to whipped egg. Add to chicken mixture and cook until egg is done. Add rice to chicken mixture, stirring constantly, and cook until rice is heated.

Ready to serve.

Cinnamon Baked Beans

Use 10-inch Dutch
Use 6 coals on bottom about 1/2 inch from edge
Use 14 coals on lid – ring edge

3 (15 ounce each) cans pork and beans (remove pieces of pork)
1/3 cup onions chopped very fine
2 level teaspoons cinnamon
1/4 cup molasses
1/2 cup dark Karo syrup
Mix together and pour into Dutch

Bake about 1 1/2 hours.

My wife was making this recipe before we were married. It has
now become a tradition to serve these beans with our baked
ham dinner. This is a quick, easy and convenient dish to take to
a potluck dinner.

Wash the Dutch in hot water using mild dish washing soap. Go to a bakery or restaurant supply store and buy a good nylon gong brush; nothing will clean better without scratching.

Fluffy White Long Grain Rice

Use 8-inch Dutch

2 1/2 cups cleaned white rice uncooked
4 cups hot water
1/2 teaspoon salt
1 teaspoon salad oil or butter

Wash rice in cold water, several minutes in a strainer, until the
talc is removed and the water is clear. Talc is the fine white
dust left on white rice after milling. Pour rice in Dutch and add
hot water, salt and oil.

Set Dutch over 15 to 16 hot coals. Place 10 hot coals on top lid.
When water starts to boil, remove all but 3 coals on bottom and
4 coals on top. Cook 15 minutes, **do not peek**.

Remove from heat and let stand for 5 to 10 minutes. Rice will
finish cooking.

Follow these directions and have perfect rice every time.

Garden Fresh Corn

Use 12-inch Dutch
Use 16 hot coals on bottom in checkerboard pattern
Bottom heat only

Fill 12-inch Dutch with small ears of fresh corn and cover with hot
water. After water comes to boil, cook for 10 minutes. When
done remove and serve with butter, salt and pepper.

German Style
Stuffed Cabbage Rolls and Sausage

Use 14-inch Dutch
Use 11 coals on bottom in checkerboard style
Use 19 coals in ring on lid

1 head green cabbage, about 3 to 4 pounds
Boiling salted water
1 pound ground German
   style sausage
1 pound lean ground beef
1 red bell pepper
   chopped fine
1 medium onion
   chopped fine
2 cups cooked white rice
1 egg
1/2 teaspoon salt
1/2 teaspoon pepper
1 can cream of mushroom
   soup
1 (14 ounce) can stewed tomatoes
1 1/2 cups milk

Remove core from cabbage. Place whole head of cabbage in 14 inch
   Dutch filled with boiling salted water. Cover and cook about 3
   minutes, or until cabbage is soft enough to pull off individual
   leaves. Repeat process often to remove all the large leaves. Lay
   each leaf flat and cut a V-shape from the thick center of each
   leaf. Chop the remaining portion of the cabbage and set aside to
   be used later.

Combine the sausage, beef, onion, rice, egg and seasonings. Mix
   thoroughly. Place a heaping tablespoon of meat mixture on each
   cabbage leaf. Tuck sides of leaf over filling while rolling leaf
   around the filling. Secure each with toothpicks.

Place the chopped cabbage on the bottom of Dutch.

Place cabbage rolls in layers on the bed of cabbage.

In a blender, mix mushroom soup, tomatoes and milk and pour over cabbage rolls. Cover and bake about 1 hour.

My wife had never eaten cabbage rolls but she knew she didn't like them because they didn't sound good to her. I had to get her to promise she would at least try them. She did and she loved them. Now we have them often.

Ham Fried Rice

Use 12-inch Dutch
Use 18 coals on bottom in checkerboard pattern
Bottom heat only

3 tablespoons oil
3 eggs lightly beaten
1 cup chopped green onion with tops
2 teaspoons finely chopped garlic
1 teaspoon finely chopped ginger root
5 cups cooked white rice
3 ounces fully cooked diced ham
3 tablespoons soy sauce
1/4 teaspoon ground white pepper

Heat 12-inch Dutch over medium heat until hot. Add 1 tablespoon oil and coat bottom of Dutch. Scramble the 3 eggs and remove from Dutch. Cut eggs into small pieces and set aside.

Place remaining 2 tablespoons of oil into Dutch and heat until hot. Add green onions, garlic and ginger root and stir-fry 1 minute. Add rice, ham, soy sauce, chopped eggs and pepper. Cook, stirring continuously until everything is thoroughly heated.

Try serving this with the *Sweet and Sour Pork* in the pork section.

Mexican Rice for
Mexican Chicken by Alma

Use 12-inch Dutch
Use 15 coals on bottom in checkerboard pattern
Bottom heat only

2 1/2 cups uncooked long grain white rice
1 tablespoon oil
Heat oil in Dutch, add rice and fry till it turns a golden brown and
  crunchy, stirring constantly.

Add
5 cups **hot** water
6 chicken bouillon cubes
    smashed
1 teaspoon cumin powder
1/4 teaspoon salt
1 teaspoon black pepper
1 tablespoon minced garlic
1 tablespoon chopped
    chives

1 medium onion chopped fine
1 cup S & W stewed original recipe tomatoes blended in blender
1 cup green bell pepper chopped fine

Simmer uncovered 15 minutes, stirring often. Remove from heat,
  cover and let stand to finish cooking, for about 15 minutes.

Serve with *Mexican Chicken* in Chicken Section and a flour or corn
  tortilla.

The Mexican Rice and Mexican Chicken recipes will make your
  family and friends think you are a professional "South of the
  Border" cook

Old Fashion Potato Bake

Use 14 inch Dutch
Use a trivet
Oven thermometer

4 14-ounce Idaho baking potatoes
2 (15-ounce each) cans chili con carne with beans
8 ounces grated sharp cheddar cheese
4 pads of butter
1 small bunch green onions chopped with tops

There are 2 ways to bake potatoes.
1. Place trivet in Dutch and preheat to 400 degrees (check with thermometer) using 21 coals on edge of lid and 11 coals on bottom. Clean potatoes and using a nail or ice pick stick a hole in potato. Bake about 45 minutes.

2. Clean and make hole in potatoes. Place potatoes on a trivet in cold Dutch. Use 26 coals on lid and 14 coals on bottom. Cooking time is about 1 hour 15 minutes for 14-ounce potato. If the potatoes are smaller, it will take less cooking time. Be sure to maintain number of coals during cooking.

Serve potatoes with butter, sour cream, green onions, chili, salt and pepper or whatever sounds good to you.

Remember you can save your unburned coals in a can to use at a later time.

This recipe turns your camp Dutch into the finest way to bake potatoes outside your kitchen. Since no food actually touches the inside of the Dutch, no washing is required. Just wipe the inside with a damp cloth, dry well and you're ready for your next meal.

Sweet Candied Yams

Use 8-inch Dutch
Use 11 coals in ring on lid
Use 5 coals on bottom

3 medium (about 2 pounds) yams
2 cups miniature marshmallows
2 tablespoons butter
3/4 cup brown sugar packed

Peel yams and par boil them until almost done, drain and set aside.

Place yams in Dutch and dot with butter. Sprinkle marshmallows over yams and sprinkle with brown sugar. Bake until marshmallows and sugar melt into a glaze.

Pinto Beans by Alma

Use 12-inch Dutch
Use 15 coals on bottom in checkerboard pattern
Bottom heat only

3 cups pinto beans
Salt and pepper to taste
1/2 teaspoon Mexican seasonings
1 teaspoon cumin powder
1/2 teaspoon minced garlic
1/4 cup chopped cilantro
1 bunch green onions using some tops thinly sliced
2 medium tomatoes diced
4 strips of bacon

Fry 4 strips of bacon in Dutch until crisp. Remove and set aside. When bacon is cold break into very small pieces. Brown the cilantro and onions in bacon grease. Remove and set aside.

Sort and clean 3 cups pinto beans and place in Dutch. Add salt, pepper, Mexican seasoning, cumin powder and minced garlic. Add enough water to cover beans.

Simmer beans making sure there is enough water to keep beans covered while cooking.

Thirty minutes before beans are done add bacon, tomatoes, onions and cilantro.

Simmer slowly until done.

These beans are a great way of cooking south of the border style and compliment such dishes as *Mexican Rice* and *Mexican Chicken*.

They can also be made into refried beans. See recipe on next page.

Refried Beans by Alma

After pinto beans are cooked, drain beans save **liquid**. Mash
  beans, leaving some bean chunks. Do not whip. Return some liquid until desired consistency is reached.

Grate some cheddar and Monterey Jack cheese and sprinkle over
  beans. Heat until cheese is melted.

Roasted Potatoes

Use 10-inch Dutch
Use a thermometer
Use 16 coals in a ring on lid
Use 7 coals on bottom in checkerboard pattern
Pre-heat Dutch to 400 degrees

5 tablespoons Grey Poupon Dijon Mustard
1/2 teaspoon Italian seasoning
2 tablespoons olive oil
1 clove of garlic chopped
6 medium small red potatoes cut into chunks

Mix mustard, Italian seasonings, olive oil and garlic in a small
  bowl.

Lightly grease Dutch and place potatoes in preheated Dutch. Add
  mustard mixture and stir till mixture coats potatoes. Bake at
  400 degrees, stir occasionally, for 35 to 40 minutes or until potatoes are fork tender.

Scalloped Potatoes

Use 10-inch Dutch
Use 16 coals in ring on lid
Use 7 coals on bottom in checkerboard pattern

3 pounds potatoes sliced very thin
1 large onion sliced very thin
1 can broccoli cheese soup
10-ounce cheddar cheese grated
Salt and pepper to taste
1 tablespoon melted butter
1/4 cup milk

Mix milk, butter and soup together in a small bowl.
Spray non-stick cooking spray in 10-inch Dutch. Place a layer of
    potatoes on bottom, then a layer of onions and sprinkle a layer
    of grated cheese on onions. Continue to alternate the layers
    until all the ingredients are used. Then pour soup mixture over
    potatoes, onions and cheese. Bake for 1 hour or until potatoes
    are tender.

Spanish Rice

Use 10-inch Dutch
Use 13 coals in ring on lid
Use 6 coals on bottom in checkerboard pattern

1/4 cup shortening
1 onion sliced very thin
1 pound ground beef
1 cup long grain white rice
2 (8 ounce each) cans tomato sauce
1 3/4 cup hot water
1 teaspoon prepared mustard
1 teaspoon salt
Pepper to taste

Melt shortening in Dutch. Add onion and brown. Add beef and
    brown. Add rice, tomato sauce, water, mustard, salt and pepper.
    Bring to boil, then simmer for about 1 hour.

Stuffed Bell Pepper

Use 14-inch Dutch
Use 18 coals in a ring on edge of lid
Use 10 coals on bottom in checkerboard pattern

3 pounds lean ground beef
6 medium red peppers
6 medium green peppers
2 1/2 cups onions – chopped
1/2 cup ketchup
1 1/2 teaspoon salt
1/2 teaspoon minced garlic
1/2 teaspoon pepper
3 (14 1/2 ounce each) cans sliced stewed tomatoes – do not drain
1 teaspoon cumin powder
3/4 cup uncooked long grain white rice

Remove top from pepper. Remove seeds and membrane. Mix
together beef, onion, rice, salt and pepper. Divide meat and rice
mixture between the 12 peppers filling each pepper equally.
Set in Dutch.

Mix cumin powder, ketchup and stewed tomatoes together and
pour over stuffed peppers.

Bake for 1 hour and 15 minutes.

Western Barbecued Bean Bake

Use 12-inch Dutch
Use 15 coals on bottom in checkerboard pattern
Bottom heat only

To make 1/2 the recipe, use 10-inch Dutch

1 pound ground lean beef
1 pound bacon cut in small pieces
1 onion chopped
1/2 cup ketchup
1/2 cup barbecue sauce
1 teaspoon salt
4 tablespoons mustard
4 tablespoons molasses
4 tablespoons brown sugar
1 teaspoon chili powder
3/4 teaspoon pepper
1 tablespoon cinnamon
2 (16-ounce each) cans red kidney beans
2 (16-ounce each) cans butter beans
2 (16-ounce each) cans pork and beans

Brown hamburger, bacon and onion together, then drain off grease.

Add rest of the ingredients and stir together well.

Simmer 1 hour. These beans make a great side dish to any meal
and are easy to prepare.

Sourdough

Sourdough Starter

2 cups all purpose flour
2 cups warm water about 95 degrees
1 package dry yeast

Combine flour and yeast then add water and mix well. Place in a
warm area overnight. The next day put 1/2 cup of starter in a
clean (scalded) jar; cover and store in refrigerator until you are
ready to use again. The remaining portion can be used immediately.

You can preheat your oven to warm and then turn it off and leave
your batter in the oven overnight.

Always use glass, crock or pottery containers for your starter.

Never use a metal container.

Never use a metal spoon in your starter.

If the starter is not going to be used for a few weeks, it may
be frozen.

Sourdough Pancakes

1 cup sourdough starter
1 cup buttermilk pancake mix
3/4 cup warm water

Mix water and starter together.

Add pancake mix.

Do not over mix. Batter will be lumpy.

Use a 14-inch Dutch lid; upside down over a lid stand with 20 hot
coals under lid to cook pancakes. Make sure lid is hot before
starting to cook.

You can also use a 12-inch or 14-inch Dutch as a skillet.
Use 15 to 16 hot coals under Dutch.

Sourdough Dinner Rolls

Old Dutch Style

Use 12-inch Dutch
Preheat lid with 18 hot coals around edge
Use 9 hot coals on bottom

2 cups warm water
2 cups bread flour
2 cups sourdough starter

Mix well, cover and set in warm place for 2 hours.

Add
2 beaten eggs
1/2 cup granulated sugar
2 teaspoon baking powder
1/2 teaspoon Saf yeast
1 teaspoon baking soda
1 teaspoon salt
3 tablespoons melted butter

Add additional flour to make a soft dough. Knead with heel of
hand until dough is smooth.

Put in bowl, cover and set in a warm place until dough doubles in
size. Pour out on floured surface and using a small cookie cutter, cut into rolls, round up and place in foil lined 12-inch
Dutch. If you lightly spray the foil with cooking oil the rolls will
be easier to remove from foil.

Cover and set in warm place until rolls double in size.

When rolls have doubled in size, set pre-heated lid on Dutch and
set Dutch over 9 hot coals.

Bake 25 to 30 minutes or until golden brown.

After rolls are baked, using a pastry brush, brush top of rolls with
melted butter.

Remove rolls from Dutch by lifting the foil.

Sourdough French Bread

Old Dutch Style

Use 14-inch Dutch
Preheat lid with 18 hot coals around edge and 3 hot coals in
   middle
Use 11 hot coals on bottom

1 1/4 cup warm water
1 level tablespoon granulated sugar
1 level tablespoon Saf yeast
2 level teaspoon salt
1 cup sourdough starter
1/2 level teaspoon baking soda
5 cups bread flour
1 tablespoon salad oil

Pour warm water into a large mixing bowl. Stir in flour, yeast,
   salt, sugar, oil, sourdough starter and soda. Mix until all liquid
   is absorbed. On a floured breadboard pour out dough mixture
   and knead until dough is smooth and elastic.

Return dough to bowl and cover until dough doubles in size.
   Divide bread dough in 2 round loaves and round up (with your
   hands form dough into a ball). Set balls in a greased 14-inch
   Dutch oven and cover. Set Dutch in a warm place. When loaves
   have doubled in size, set preheated lid on Dutch and place
   Dutch on 11 hot coals.

Bake for 45 minutes or until golden brown.

**Never store sourdough starter in a metal
container and never stir it with a metal spoon.**

Bread, rolls and biscuits

Baking Powder Biscuits

Modern Dutch Style

Use 14-inch Dutch oven
Oven thermometer
Trivet
10-inch cake pan
Use 12 coals on bottom in
    checkerboard pattern
Use 23 coals on lid
Preheat lid

2 cups cake flour
5 teaspoons baking powder
1/2 teaspoon salt
3 teaspoons granulated sugar
1/2 teaspoon cream of tartar
1/2 cup shortening
3/4 cup milk

Mixing by hand:

Sift all the dry ingredients into a large mixing bowl. Mix in short-
    ening with palm of hand until it is the texture of breadcrumbs.
    Add milk and mix together until milk is absorbed. Roll out on
    floured breadboard 1 inch thick and cut with a 2-inch biscuit
    cutter. Bake in a 10-inch cake pan that has been sprayed with a
    no stick cooking spray.

Place trivet in Dutch and preheat to 450 degrees. Use the ther-
    mometer to check heat. Place biscuits in cake pan, brush with
    equal parts egg and milk beaten place in Dutch and bake about
    20 to 22 minutes.

For a lighter biscuit, follow the above directions and mix in a
    mixer about 1 1/2 minutes. Roll out, cut and bake.

Cinnamon Rolls

Modern Dutch Style

Use 14-inch Dutch
Thermometer
10-inch cake pan
Trivet
Use 11 coals on bottom in
    checkerboard pattern
Ring lid with 21 coals
Preheat lid

1/2 cup sugar
1 teaspoon salt
3 eggs
4 tablespoons **instant** powdered milk
4 cups bread flour
1 cup cake flour
1 teaspoon cinnamon
1/2 cup shortening
1 teaspoon pure vanilla
3 **level** tablespoons Saf yeast
1 1/2 cups water

Mixing with an electric mixer:
Mix ingredients same as by hand, then mix at a medium speed
    about 8 to 10 minutes or till dough becomes elastic and smooth.

Mixing by hand:
Mix all the dry ingredients together. Add vanilla, eggs and water.
    Mix together until the dry ingredients are wet. Turn out on a
    floured breadboard. Knead with heel of hand till dough is elas-
    tic. Place dough back in bowl, cover and set in warm area until
    dough doubles in size. Next you roll dough on a floured bread-
    board about 1/4 inch thick and about 12 inches wide.

Brush entire top of dough with egg wash. **See recipe for egg
wash in Miscellaneous section**.

Sprinkle dough with raisins and then a mixture of cinnamon and sugar. (This is in addition to what is listed above)

Roll dough into shape of a log. On the last roll, brush dough with egg wash and press to seal edge of dough. Cut dough about 2 inches wide and place in cake pan with raisin side down and flatten with fingers so they are all the same height. Wash tops with egg wash, cover and set aside in a warm area till rolls have doubled in side. Pre-heat your Dutch, with trivet inside to 385 degrees. Bake about 12 to 15 minutes, till golden brown. Remove rolls from pan to cool.

Icing for Cinnamon Rolls

2 cups powdered sugar
1/4 teaspoon pure vanilla
1 tablespoon soft butter
Pinch of salt

Add enough cold water to make icing very thin. Drizzle icing over cinnamon rolls.

Cinnamon Rolls

Old Dutch Style

Use 10-inch Dutch oven
Use 7 coals on bottom in checkerboard pattern
Use 16 coals to ring lid
Preheat lid

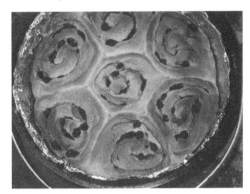

1/2 cup sugar
1 teaspoon salt
3 eggs
4 tablespoons **instant**
  powered milk
4 cups bread flour
1 cup cake flour
1 teaspoon cinnamon
1/2 cup shortening
1 teaspoon pure vanilla
3 **level** tablespoons Saf yeast
1 1/2 cup water

Mixing with an electric mixer:
Mix ingredients same as by hand, then mix at a medium speed
  about 8 to 10 minutes or till dough becomes elastic and smooth.

Mixing by hand:
Mix all the dry ingredients together. Add vanilla, eggs and water.
  Mix together until the dry ingredients are wet. Turn out on a
  floured breadboard. Knead with heel of hand till dough is elastic. Place dough back in bowl, cover and in set in warm area
  until dough doubles in size. Next you roll dough on a floured
  breadboard about 1/4 inch thick and about 12 inches wide.

Brush entire top of dough with egg wash. **See recipe for egg
  wash in Miscellaneous section**.

Sprinkle dough with raisins and then a mixture of cinnamon and
  sugar. (This is in addition to what is listed above.)

Roll dough into shape of a log. On the last roll, brush dough with
  egg wash and press to seal edge of dough. Cut dough about 2
  inches wide.

Have your 10-inch Dutch lined with foil coming up the side almost to the top. Spray lightly inside foil with a no stick cooking oil. As you are cutting the rolls, lay them in the foil. Flatten the rolls so they are level. Brush the tops of the rolls with egg wash. Cover with a cloth; set the Dutch in a warm area till the rolls have doubled in size. At this time place the Dutch over the 7 hot coals and set the pre-heated lid on Dutch. Bake about 23 minutes or until golden brown. Remove Dutch from coals and remove rolls by lifting the foil from the Dutch. Let cool.

Icing for cinnamon rolls
2 cups powdered sugar
1/4 teaspoon pure vanilla
1 tablespoon soft butter
Pinch of salt

Add enough cold water to make icing very thin. Drizzle icing over cinnamon rolls.

Dinner Rolls

Modern Dutch Style

Use 14-inch Dutch
Trivet
Oven thermometer
2 10-inch cake pan
Use 11 coals on bottom in checkerboard pattern
Use 21 coals on edge of lid
Preheat lid

1/4 cup sugar
2 3/4 cups bread flour
1/4 cup shortening
1/4 cup instant powdered milk
2 teaspoons salt **level teaspoons**
2 tablespoons Saf yeast **level tablespoons**
1 1/4 cup water

Mixing by hand:
Put all the dry ingredients in bowl and blend together. Add liquid
and mix till the liquid is absorbed. Pour mixture on floured
breadboard. Knead with heel of hand till dough is elastic and
smooth. Return to bowl, cover and place in warm area till
dough doubles in size. Return dough to floured breadboard and
cut dough into 24 equal size pieces. Round them up (see terminology) and place them evenly in 2 ten-inch cake pans, which
have been greased. Cover pans and place in warm area till rolls
doubles in size.

Place the trivet in Dutch, check with oven thermometer to reach
400 degrees. When rolls have doubled in size remove thermometer and place inside a pan of rolls. Replace lid and bake for 10
to 12 minutes, or until golden brown. Remove rolls from pan;
place them on a wire rack and brush top of rolls with melted
butter while rolls are still warm.

Mixing by machine:
Mix as in directions above and mix at medium speed until dough
becomes elastic and smooth, about 10 minutes. Continue as
instructed above.

This dough can be used for Parker House Rolls, Twin Rolls or any
shape of dinner roll you may want to make. When kept in a zip
lock bag, these rolls will stay fresh, for a short time.

Dinner Rolls

Old Dutch Style

Use 2 10-inch Dutch ovens
Use 7 coals on bottom in checkerboard pattern
Use 16 coals in ring on lid – Preheat lid
Line Dutch with foil to top
    edge
Spray inside foil with a no
    stick cooking spray

2 3/4 cups bread flour
1/4 cup granulated sugar
1/4 cup instant powered
    milk
1/4 cup shortening
2 **level** teaspoons salt
2 **level** tablespoons Saf
    Yeast
1 1/4 cups water

Mixing by Hand:
Put all the dry ingredients in a bowl and blend together. Add liquid and mix till the liquid is absorbed. Pour mixture on floured
breadboard. Knead with heel of hand till dough is elastic and
smooth. Return to bowl, cover and place in warm area till
dough doubles in size. Return dough to floured breadboard and
cut dough into 24 equal size pieces. Round them up (see terminology) and place them evenly in the foil, 12 rolls to a Dutch

oven, cover with towel and set in warm place till rolls double in size. When rolls have doubled in size, set Dutch on 7 hot coals, place pre-heated lid on Dutch and bake for 30 to 35 minutes, or until golden brown. By lifting the foil, remove the rolls. Place on wire rack and brush with melted butter while still warm.

Remove Dutch from coals after 20 minutes of cooking and finish cooking with top heat only.

Machine mixing:
Place all the ingredients in bowl and mix at medium speed about 10 minutes, or until dough in elastic and smooth.

The ideal temperature for any yeast raised dough, right after it has been mixed, is 80 degrees F. If the dough is either too warm or too cold you will not get the best results. You should always cover the dough with a piece of plastic.

Grandma's Country Corn Bread

Old Dutch Style

Use 10-inch Dutch
Use 6 coals on bottom
Ring lid with about 14 coals –
    preheat lid
Line Dutch with foil up sides
    close to edge
Spray foil with no stick cooking
    spray

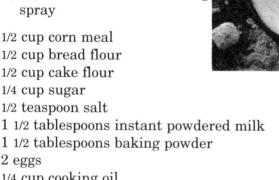

1/2 cup corn meal
1/2 cup bread flour
1/2 cup cake flour
1/4 cup sugar
1/2 teaspoon salt
1 1/2 tablespoons instant powdered milk
1 1/2 tablespoons baking powder
2 eggs
1/4 cup cooking oil
1/4 cup water

Mix ingredients as listed. Pour into Dutch, which has been lined
    with foil and sprayed with a no stick cooking spray. Set Dutch
    on 6 hot coals and place preheated lid on Dutch. Bake for about
    12 minutes, or until golden brown. Remove from heat, lifting
    foil remove cornbread. Serve with honey, jelly, butter or eat
    plain.

Any cornbread left over may be used in stuffing your
    Cornish game hen.

Ranch bread

Old Dutch Style

Use 14-inch Dutch
Use 12 coals on bottom in checkerboard pattern
Use 22 coals, 18 in ring on lid and 4 coals in middle – pre-heated

1-1/3 cup warm water
3 cups bread flour
1/2 cup dry instant potatoes
3 **level** tablespoons sugar
1 **level** tablespoon salt
2 **level** tablespoons shortening
3 **level** tablespoons instant powered milk
1 1/2 **level** tablespoons Saf Yeast

Mixing by Hand.
Place all dry ingredients in a bowl, add liquid and mix together.
Place dough on floured breadboard and knead with heel of hand
till dough is elastic and smooth. Return dough to bowl, cover
with cloth and place in warm area. When dough has doubled in
size, place dough on floured breadboard and round up (see terminology) into a ball. Cover and let set for about 15 minutes.
Then round up dough, the second time, into a ball and place
into a 14-inch Dutch that has been lined with foil and sprayed
lightly with no stick cooking spray. Sprinkle the top of dough
with 1 additional teaspoon of ground instant potatoes. Cover
Dutch and set in warm area until dough doubles in size. When
dough has doubled, place Dutch over 12 hot coals and place pre-
heated lid on Dutch. Don't peek for at least 30 minutes. Bread
should bake in 30 to 40 minutes. Be sure to have enough hot
coals to maintain temperature.

**After baking for 25 minutes, remove Dutch from bottom
coals and finish baking with top heat only.**

Machine mixing:
Measure, into a bowl, all the ingredients as in directions above. At
medium speed, mix about 10 minutes or until dough is elastic
and smooth. Continue as instructed above.

Grandma Smith's Old Fashion Biscuits

Old Dutch Style

Use 10-inch Dutch
Use 9 coals on bottom in checkerboard pattern
Ring lid with 16 coals with 3 coals in middle – preheat lid
Line Dutch with foil almost to edge
Spray foil lightly with no stick cooking spray

2 cups cake flour
5 **level** teaspoons baking
    powder
1/2 teaspoon salt
3 teaspoons sugar
1/2 teaspoon cream of tartar
1/2 cup shortening
3/4 cup milk

Sift all the dry ingredients in
    large mixing bowl. Mix in
shortening with palm of hand until texture of course corn meal,
then add milk, mix until milk is absorbed. Roll out dough on
lightly floured breadboard about 1 inch think and cut with 2-
inch biscuit cutter.

Place biscuits in Dutch oven lined with foil and sprayed lightly
with a no stick cooking spray. Before baking brush biscuits with
equal parts egg and milk mixture that has been well beaten.
Place Dutch on hot coals. Place lid on Dutch and bake 15 to 17
minutes or until golden brown.

For a lighter biscuit, mix with electric mixer at medium speed
    about 1 1/2 minutes.
Remove biscuits by lifting edges of foil from Dutch.

As a child, I can remember having biscuits and country gravy at
    least once a week for breakfast. It was a wonderful time.

Corn Tortillas

2 cups Quaker Masa Harina mix
1 1/8 cup tap water

Mix together well
If mixture feels too dry, add 1 or 2 tablespoons water

Divide dough into 16 equal size balls, cover with towel and let
   rest 20 minutes.
Roll each out flat or use tortilla press. Fry on 14-inch hot Dutch
   lid, ungreased, each side 15 to 30 seconds.

Flour Tortillas

4 cups all purpose flour
1 teaspoon baking powder
2 teaspoons salt
1/3 cup salad oil

Mix together well
Add 1 2/3 to 2 cups hot water

Mix flour tortillas into dough, then divide into round balls about
   the size of golf balls.
Cover and let rest covered for 20 minutes. Roll each out flat or use
   a tortilla press. Fry on 14-inch hot Dutch lid, ungreased, heat
   and turn once

Corn or flour tortillas are great when served with *Mexican Rice* by
   Alma and *Mexican Chicken* by **Alma**. They are delicious when
   served with *South of the Border Ox Tail Soup* by **Imelda**.

White Bread

Modern Dutch style
Use 14-inch Dutch
Use 12 coals on bottom in checkerboard pattern
Use 18 coals in ring on lid with another 4 coals in middle
  – preheat lid
Oven thermometer
Trivet
10-inch pie pan

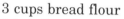

3 cups bread flour
3 **level** tablespoons
  granulated sugar
1 **level** tablespoon salt
2 **level** tablespoons shortening
3 **level** tablespoons instant powered milk
1 1/2 **level** tablespoons Saf Yeast
1 1/3 cups warm water

Hand mixing:
Blend well together all the ingredients except water. Add water
  and mix. Turn out on a floured breadboard. Knead with heel of
  hand till dough is elastic and smooth. Put dough into bowl,
  cover and place in a warm area until dough has doubled in size.
  Turn out on floured breadboard and round up (see terminology)
  into a ball, cover and let rest for 15 minutes. Again round up
  dough into a ball and place it into a greased 10-inch pie pan.
  Cover and set in a warm place until dough doubles in size.

Pre-heat Dutch oven to 425 degrees, check with thermometer.
Check heat as quickly as possible to maintain temperature.

Place the dough, in the pie pan in the Dutch and bake for 35 to 40
  minutes. Do not peek the first 30 minutes. Place bread on a
  wire rack to cool and brush top with melted
  butter.

Machine mixing:
Mix all the ingredients together at medium speed about 10 minutes or until the dough is elastic and smooth. Handle as above.

White Bread

Old Dutch style
Use 14-inch Dutch
Use 12 coals on bottom in checkerboard pattern
Use 18 coals in ring on lid with 4 coals in middle – preheated

3 cups bread flour
3 **level** tablespoons sugar
1 **level** tablespoon salt
2 **level** tablespoons
   shortening
3 **level** tablespoons
   instant powered milk
1 1/2 **level** tablespoons
   Saf Yeast
1 1/3 cups warm water

Hand mixing:
Mix all ingredients together, adding water last. Turn out dough on
floured breadboard and knead with heel of hand until dough in
elastic and smooth. Return dough to bowl, cover and set in a
warm area until dough doubles in size. Turn dough out onto a
flour breadboard and round up (see terminology) into a ball.
Cover and let rest 15 minutes. Again, round up into a ball and
place in a greased Dutch oven. Cover with a towel and set
Dutch in a warm area until dough doubles in size. Place Dutch
over 12 hot coals and place preheated lid on Dutch and bake 35
to 40 minutes.

**After baking 25 minutes, remove Dutch from bottom heat
and finish cooking with top heat only.**

Place bread on wire rack to cool and brush top with melted butter

Machine mixing:
Mix all ingredients at medium speed for 10 minutes, or until
dough becomes elastic and smooth. Handle as above.

Baking white bread in a camp Dutch, in the back country where
the fresh air is mingled with the aroma of fresh baked bread, is
one of the greatest experiences in life.

Whole Wheat Bread

Modern Dutch style
Use 14-inch Dutch
Use 12 coals on bottom in checkerboard pattern
Use 18 coals in ring on lid with another 4 coals in middle – pre-
    heated
Trivet
Oven thermometer
10-inch pie pan

1 1/2 cup whole wheat flour
1 1/2 cup white bread flour
1 **level** tablespoon salt
3 **level** tablespoons granulated sugar
3 **level** tablespoons instant powdered milk
2 **level** tablespoons shortening
1 1/2 **level** tablespoons Saf Yeast
1 1/3 cups warm water

Hand mixing:
Mix all ingredients together in bowl, add water and mix again.
    Place dough on a floured breadboard and knead with heel of
    hand till dough is elastic and smooth. Return dough to bowl,
    cover and place in a warm area until dough doubles in size. Put
    dough on floured breadboard and round up (see terminology)
    into a ball. Cover and let rest for 15 minutes. Round up again
    and place dough in a 10-inch greased pie pan. Cover and place
    in warm area until dough doubles in size.

After dough has doubled in size and Dutch has been heated to 425
    degrees, place dough in pan on trivet and bake 35 to 40 min-
    utes. Do not peek for the first 30 minutes.

Place bread on wire rack to cool and brush top with melted butter

Machine mixing:
Measure all ingredients into a bowl and mix at medium speed for
    10 minutes or until dough is elastic and smooth. Handle as
    above.

Whole Wheat Bread

Old Dutch style
Use 14-inch Dutch
Use 12 coals on bottom in checkerboard pattern
Use 18 coals in a ring on lid with another 4 coals in center – pre
  heated

1 1/2 cups whole wheat flour
1 1/2 cups white bread flour
1 1/2 **level** tablespoons Saf Yeast
1 **level** tablespoon salt
3 **level** tablespoons granulated sugar
3 **level** tablespoons instant powdered milk
2 **level** tablespoons shortening
1 1/3 cups warm water

Hand mixing:
Blend all ingredients in a bowl, adding water last. Mix all together. Pour out on a floured breadboard. Knead with heel of hand
  till dough is elastic and smooth. Place dough back into bowl,
  cover and place in warm area until dough doubles in size. Then
  place dough on a floured breadboard and round up (see terminology) into a ball. Cover dough and let rest for 15 minutes.
  Again round up dough in a ball and place dough in a greased
  14-inch Dutch, cover with towel and set in warm area until
  dough doubles in size. Place Dutch over hot coals and place pre-
  heated lid on Dutch, bake for 35 to 40 minutes. Do not peek for
  first 30 minutes.

**After baking 25 minutes, remove Dutch from bottom coals
  and finish baking with top heat only.**

Place on wire rack to cool and brush top with butter.

Machine mixing:
Mix all the ingredients at medium speed for 10 minutes, or until
  dough is elastic and smooth. Handle as above.

Notes

Cakes, cobblers and pies

Apple Brown Betty

Old Dutch Style

Use 10-inch Dutch Oven
Pre heat lid with 14 hot
   coals around edge
Use 6 coals in checker-
   board pattern on the
   bottom

10 Granny Smith apples
   peeled, cored and
   sliced
1 cube melted butter
1/2 teaspoon salt
2 teaspoons cinnamon
1/4 teaspoon nutmeg
1 cup brown sugar
1/2 cup raisins
1/4 cup apple cider
3 cups toasted bread cut into cubes
1 lemon – squeeze juice from a lemon

Mix apples, raisins, brown sugar, cinnamon, nutmeg, and salt in a
   bowl. Pour melted butter and lemon over bread cubes. Put a
   thin layer of apple mixture on bottom of 10-inch Dutch.

Toss remaining apples and bread cubes together. Fill Dutch.

Set Dutch on 6 coals placed in a checkerboard pattern. Set pre-
   heated Dutch lid on Dutch oven and bake 30 to 35 minutes.

This recipe will work with dried apples. Be sure to use a good
   quality apple. Soak the apples overnight in water. Every 1
   pound of apples will soak up 2 quarts of hot water.

Apple Crisp

Old Dutch style

Use 10-inch Dutch
Preheat lid with 15 coals hot coals around edge with 4 coals
    in middle of lid
Use 6 hot coals in checkerboard pattern on the bottom

Filling:

2 cans (1 lb. 5 ounces each) apple pie filling
1/2 cup brown raisins
juice from 1 lemon

Pour filling, apples, raisins and lemon juice into a 10 inch Dutch
    oven.

Topping:

1 1/2 cubes soft butter	This is the first stage
1/2 cup white sugar	cream together. Use a
1/2 cup brown sugar	separate bowl to mix the
1/2 teaspoon soda	first stage.
1/4 teaspoon salt	
1/4 teaspoon vanilla	
1/2 teaspoon cinnamon	

This is the second stage:

Using a separate bowl blend together
1/2 cup quick oats
1/2 cup chopped walnuts or pecans
1 1/2 cup all purpose white flour

Add the second stage into the first stage and mix with fingers
    until it is a mealy texture.

After fully mixed, pour over apple mixture.

Set Dutch on the 6 hot coals and set preheated lid on Dutch.
    Bake for 40 minutes.

Don't peek.

Black Forest Torte with Brandy

Old Dutch Style

Use 12-inch Dutch
Preheat lid with 16 hot coals around edge
Use 8 hot coals in checkerboard pattern on the bottom

2 cans (21 ounces each) cherry pie filling
1 devils food cake mix (any brand)
1/4 cup Kirschwasser (cherry brandy)

Line a 12-inch Dutch oven with foil.

In a bowl mix cherry filling and brandy mixture.

In bowl mix cake mix according to directions on package.

Pour cherry mixture into lined Dutch oven.

Pour cake batter over cherry mixture.

Set Dutch over 8 hot coals. Set preheated lid on Dutch and bake
20 to 25 minutes.

To tell if the cake is done, insert a toothpick in cake, if it comes out
clean cake is done.

Serve with ice cream or chocolate sauce.

This is a favorite with lots of chocolate sauce. A chocolate
lover's dream.

Cherry Crisp

Old Dutch Style

Use 10-inch Dutch
Preheat lid with 15 coals around edge and 4 coals in middle
Use 6 coals in checkerboard pattern on the bottom

Filling:
2 cans (21 ounces each) cherry pie filling
Juice from 1 lemon
Mix cherries and lemon juice and pour directly into Dutch oven

Topping:
1 1/2 cups cake flour
1/2 cup quick oats
1/4 teaspoon salt
1/2 cup brown sugar
1/2 cup white sugar
1 1/2 cubes soft butter
1/2 teaspoon baking soda
1/2 cup chopped pecans

Cream together butter, salt, soda, brown sugar and white sugar.

Mix oats, flour and nuts into creamed butter mixture.

Sprinkle over cherries.

Set Dutch over the 6 hot coals and set preheated lid on Dutch.

Cook for 45 minutes, until brown.

Cherry Cobbler with Bisquick

Modern Dutch style

Use 12-inch Dutch
Use a 10-inch cake pan
A trivet
An oven thermometer
Use 9 hot coals in checkerboard pattern on bottom
Ring the edge of lid with 17 hot coals

1 pound pie dough
2 cans (21 ounces each) cherry pie filling
2 cups Bisquick
1 1/2 cups milk
1 teaspoon vanilla

Line one 10-inch cake pan with pie dough.
Add cherries

In separate bowl, mix Bisquick and milk together until
consistency of cake batter. Spoon over cherry mixture.

Place trivet in Dutch. Place oven thermometer in Dutch.

Place Dutch over hot coals with the lid lined with hot coals. Preheat Dutch to 400 degrees. When it reaches 400 degrees,
remove thermometer and place cake pan in oven and bake for
45 minutes to 1 hour or until top is golden brown.

Cherry Cobbler with Bisquick

Old Dutch style

Use 10-inch Dutch oven
Pre-heat lid with 16 coals around edge
Use 6 hot coals in checkerboard pattern on the bottom

2 cans (1 pound 5 ounces each) cherry pie filling

Line 10-inch Dutch with foil and pour cherries directly into Dutch

Mix together, until it becomes the consistency of cake batter
2 cups baking mix
1 1/2 cups milk
1 teaspoon vanilla

Spoon over cherries.

Set Dutch over hot coals and place pre-heated lid on Dutch.
Bake 25 to 30 minutes or until golden brown.

This is a quick and easy treat on any camping trip. It's easy to
serve right from the Dutch, be sure to use a wooden spoon as
not to scratch the seasoning in your Dutch oven.

Cherry Dutch Pie

Modern Dutch Style

Use 12-inch Dutch oven
One 9-inch pie pan
A trivet
An oven thermometer
Use 9 hot coals on bottom
Ring the edge of lid with 14 hot coals and 4 in middle

1 can (21 ounces) cherry
    pie filling
9 ounce pie dough

Line pie pan with pie
    dough.
Pour cherry filling into
    pie pan.

Topping
Cream together
1/2 cup granulated sugar
1 cup butter
Add 2 cups cake flour and mix until mealy.

Place trivet and thermometer in Dutch.

Set Dutch on hot coals. Place lid on Dutch. Preheat Dutch to 400
    degrees. Remove thermometer and place pie pan with cherries
    inside Dutch. Bake about 45 minutes.

Remove 3 coals from bottom heat.

Sprinkle topping over cherries.

Replace lid, with hot coals, on Dutch. Using top heat only, bake
    until golden brown, about 10 minutes.

This recipe also works well with apple filling.

Chocolate Upside Down Cake
Old Dutch Style

Use 12-inch Dutch
Pre-heat lid with 17 hot coals on edge
Use 9 hot coals in checkerboard pattern on bottom

1/4 cup honey
3/4 cup brown sugar
1 1/2 cups chopped walnuts or pecans
1/2 cube melted butter
1 package chocolate cake mix

Line a 12-inch Dutch with foil, bringing the foil up on the sides at least 3 inches. Sprinkle the brown sugar on bottom. Pour melted butter over sugar, then spoon honey over sugar and butter. Sprinkle the nuts evenly over sugar mixture.

Mix the cake according to directions on the box. Pour cake batter into Dutch.

Set the Dutch over 9 hot coals and place pre-heated lid on Dutch. Bake about 40 minutes or until a toothpick comes out clean.

Remove the cake by lifting the foil from the Dutch and **immediately** turn upside down on a flat surface. Remove foil and let cool at least 10 minutes.

Icing:
3 cups powdered sugar
1 square melted semi-sweet bakers chocolate
1/4 teaspoon salt
1/4 teaspoon vanilla
1 tablespoon butter
milk as needed

Melt chocolate and butter in small Dutch. Add salt, vanilla and powdered sugar. Mix together. Thin with milk to make icing thin enough to drizzle over cake.

After cake has cooled for 10 minutes, drizzle the chocolate icing over the cake.
Serve with ice cream, whipped cream or Cool Whip.

Dutch Peach Pie

Modern Dutch Style

Use 14-inch Dutch
One 9-inch deep pie pan
A trivet
An oven thermometer
Ring top edge of lid with 17 hot coals and 4 in middle of lid
Use 11 hot coals in checkerboard pattern on bottom

9-ounce pie dough
Line pie pan with pie dough

Filling:
4 cans (15 ounces) sliced peaches
1 tablespoon sugar
1 tablespoon white flour
Drain peaches

Mix sugar and flour together, add 1/4 cup juice. Let set 5
    minutes then fold into peaches.

Topping:
1/2 cup granulated sugar
1 cube soft butter
2 cups all purpose flour
1/4 teaspoon nutmeg

Cream sugar and butter together; add flour and nutmeg and
    mix until mealy.

Put trivet and thermometer into Dutch. Place Dutch on hot coals
    then place lid on Dutch. Heat to 400 degrees.

Pour peach mixture into lined pie pan. Heat the Dutch to 400
    degrees, remove thermometer and place pie pan on trivet. Bake
    for 45 minutes. Remove all but 6 hot coals from bottom of
    Dutch. Sprinkle topping on pie, return lid and continue to bake
    about 10 minutes, until top is golden brown.

Lattice Top Cherry Pie

Old Dutch Style

Use 10-inch Dutch

Preheat lid with 12 hot
  coals on edge and 4 hot
  coals in the
  middle

Use 6 hot coals in checkerboard pattern on bottom

16-ounces of pie dough
1 lemon

2 cans (21 ounces each)
  cherry pie filling

Roll out pie dough for bottom crust

Line bottom of Dutch with pie dough bringing it up the side about
  2 inches high.

Pour the 2 cans of pie filling into a bowl. Add the juice of 1 lemon
  for extra tartness. Blend together well and let stand 10 minutes. Pour cherry mixture into Dutch.

Roll out remaining pie dough and cut into strips about 1 inch
  wide. Leaving a small space between the strips, lay the strips
  crisscross over the cherry mixture to form a lattice top.

Set Dutch over the 6 hot coals and place pre-heated lid on Dutch.
  Bake for 1 hour.

Every 15 minutes turn Dutch a quarter turn over coals. Then turn
  lid a quarter turn on Dutch to guarantee even heating.

Have extra hot coals on hand to maintain 16 full size coals on top
  and 6 on bottom during baking.

This is especially delicious when served with ice cream.

Peach Crisp

Old Dutch Style

Use 10-inch Dutch
Pre-heat lid with 15 hot coals at edge of led and 4 hot
    coals in middle

Use 6 hot coals on bottom in checkerboard pattern

Filling:
4 cans (15 ounces each) of peaches drained

Topping:
1 1/2 cups cake flour
1/2 cup quick oats
1/4 teaspoon salt
1/2 cup brown sugar
1/2 cup granulated sugar
1 1/2 cube soft butter
1/2 teaspoon baking soda
1/2 cup chopped pecans
1/2 teaspoon nutmeg

Cream together butter, salt, soda, brown sugar, nutmeg and
    granulated sugar.

Mix oats, flour and pecans into creamed butter mixture.
    Sprinkle over peaches.

Set Dutch over 6 hot coals and place preheated lid on Dutch.

Bake for 40 minutes or until golden brown.

Pie Dough

Makes pie crust for one 9- inch 2 crust pie or about one pound of
pie dough

2 1/2 cups all purpose flour
1/2 cup Crisco
1 cube soft butter
1/2 teaspoon salt
1 teaspoon granulated sugar
1 teaspoon vinegar
1 egg whipped
1/4 cup ice water

In a bowl mix shortening and butter to a smooth paste.

Add flour and blend until mealy.

In separate bowl mix egg, ice water, salt, vinegar and sugar.

Pour liquid mixture into flour mixture.

Mix well – **be careful don't over mix.**

Chill before rolling out piecrust.

If the piecrust is chilled it will roll out easier.

This pie dough can be made ahead and will keep in the refrigerator for a week or in the freezer for 2 months. In either case,
wrap it will in a plastic wrap. For the freezer use the plastic
wrap and then wrap in foil. I always have frozen pie dough in
my freezer because I never know when I may want a quick
dessert.

Pineapple Cherry Dump Cake

Old Dutch Style

Use 12-inch Dutch
Preheat lid with 14 hot coals on rim and 2 hot coals in
center of lid
Use 6 hot coals on bottom

1 (21-ounce can) cherry pie filling
1 tablespoon lemon juice
1 (21-ounce can) crushed pineapple – **do not drain**
1 package white or yellow cake mix
1 cube melted butter
1/2 cup chopped walnuts

Grease 12-inch Dutch with solid vegetable shortening.

Mix cherry pie filling and lemon juice together and pour
into Dutch.

Pour pineapple on top of cherry mixture.

Sprinkle dry cake mix on top of pineapple then drizzle melted butter on cake mix.

Sprinkle nuts on top of the cake mix.

Set Dutch on hot coals, place preheated lid on Dutch and bake 30
minutes or until golden brown.

Will serve 8 to 12.

This cake is a favorite with my grandchildren. I start the coals and
they finish and bake the cake. This is an easy recipe for a Dutch
oven lesson for kids.

Pineapple Upside Down Cake

Old Dutch Style

Use 12-inch Dutch

Preheat lid with 17 hot coals on
   edge
Use 9 hot coals in checkerboard
   pattern on bottom

1 (20-ounce can) of pineapple
   slices **drained**
1/2 cube melted butter
1/4 cup honey
3/4 cup brown sugar
Maraschino cherries without stems
1 package yellow cake mix

Line the 12-inch Dutch with foil, bringing the foil up on the sides
   at least 3 inches.

Sprinkle the brown sugar on bottom; pour melted butter over
   sugar and next spoon the honey over sugar and butter. Place
   the pineapple slices on above mixture. Place a maraschino cherry, which had been dried on a paper towel, in center of each
   pineapple slice.

Mix cake mix according to directions on the box. Pour batter over
   fruit. Set Dutch over 9 hot coals and place preheated lid on
   Dutch. Bake about 40 minutes or until a toothpick comes out
   clean. Remove by lifting foil from Dutch. Roll sides of foil down
   around cake and immediately turn upside down on a flat surface. Remove foil.

You may use cherries or peaches in place of pineapple by following
   directions below:
1 (29-ounce) can drained peach slices
1 (21-ounce) can cherry pie filling

Follow the instructions as if using pineapple, except omit the
   maraschino cherries.

Pineapple Upside Down Cake

Modern Dutch Style

Use 12-inch Dutch
Two 8-inch cake pans
A trivet
An oven thermometer
Preheat lid with 17 hot coals on edge of lid
Use 9 hot coals on bottom

1 (20-ounce) can pineapple slices – **drained**
1 package yellow cake mix
1/2   cube butter
2   rounded tablespoons brown sugar
3   tablespoons honey
Maraschino cherries without stems

Grease each 8-inch cake pan with 1/4 cube butter. Sprinkle each
    pan with 1 tablespoon brown sugar and spoon 1 tablespoon
    honey on bottom.

Place pineapple slices on bottom of each pan.

Wipe the maraschino cherries dry on a paper towel and place one
    in the center of each pineapple slice.

Mix cake mix as instructed on package.
Pour cake mix evenly over pineapple in both pans.

Place trivet in Dutch oven with a thermometer. Preheat Dutch to
    375 degrees, using amount of hot coals as described above. Once
    your Dutch has reached desired temperature remove
    thermometer and place a cake pan inside Dutch. Bake 25 to 30
    minutes or until a toothpick comes out clean.

Remove cake pan and turn upside down **immediately** on a flat
    surface. Gently remove cake pan from cake.

To bake the second cake repeat the entire process beginning with
    preheating the oven and checking with an oven thermometer.

This is one of the easiest, best tasting and beautiful cakes you
    will ever make in a Dutch oven.

FIRELESS COOKER

The term fireless cooker brings to mind some way to cook without fire. The following story is just that, a way of cooking without fire.

My grandmother, when cooking or baking, always went into great detail to describe how and why she would do different things in preparing food. I started working at age 12 in a bakery and I believe this detailing of how and why was part of my motivation to become a baker. My grandmother told me about a box that grandpa had made her so she could cook some of her meat out doors. I remember her, very clearly, telling me about the box but that is all I remembered until one day, while doing research for this book, I came across an old recipe book detailing such a fireless cooker. This article brought back my memory of the story my grandmother had told me about the box and an old iron pot she used in it. Being curious and always looking for new ways to use my camp Dutch I revised the directions found in the old cook book since I couldn't find any excelsior. Excelsior was thin wood shaving used many years ago to stuff mattresses, chairs and even car seats in the 1920's. Not having excelsior I turned to modern age insulation. Using plywood I made a wooden box (cabinet), 24 inches long, 24 inches wide and 24 inches deep and also made a bottom and a top lid. On all the sides, bottom and top I glued 2-inch foam insulation. Keep in mind, if the hot pot touches the foam insulation, the insulation will melt. Next I poured 6 inches of sawdust over the bottom. Next I sat a 12-inch Dutch oven on the sawdust, full of stew which I had brought to a hard boil for 15 minutes. Making sure the lid was well seated I poured sawdust over and around the Dutch until it was completely covered. I put the lid on top of the box and waited 4 hours. When I removed the Dutch from the box, the stew was completely cooked. If the stew is not hot enough, it can be reheated to desired temperature.

I have enclosed the article on fireless cookers, which brought back the story my grandmother had told me and sparked my curiosity. I have included some of the recipes and a cooking chart.

If you have more time on your hands than you know what to do with, or if you are just a little curious like me, you may want to try the fireless cooker. It won't compare with regular Dutch oven cooking and it will never replace the microwave, but at one time in history it was what we call today "a big deal".

The following article is taken from a 1916 Calumet Baking Powder cookbook:

FIRELESS COOKERS

The use of the fireless cooker is spreading rapidly on account of its saving in fuel, time, work and worry. It consists of a box or chest packed with a good non-conductor of heat, into which a kettle containing the food heated to the boiling point, is placed. The lid, consisting of the same non-conducting material, is closed, and the heat cannot escape, consequently the water in the kettle remains at the boiling point for several hours, and the food in the water is bound to cook the same as if it were on the stove.

These cookers are now being manufactured by many firms. Some of them, however, are not as good as home-made ones. A fireless cooker can easily be made by packing excelsior in a square box or bushel basket tightly around the kettle to be used, and on removing the kettle, cotton cloth can be placed over the excelsior and tacked to remain, and a cushion of excelsior made to fit over the top. About three inches of excelsior should be left solid on the bottom, and the sides of the box lined with newspapers before putting the excelsior therein. About four inches of excelsior should be left between the kettle and the sides of the box, and the same kettle should always be used so as to fit snugly in its own nest.

In the fireless cooker, there is no evaporation. All the goodness and flavor of the food is retained by this slow and thorough mode of cooking. Onions and cabbage may be cooked without the odor permeating the house. While doing the dinner dishes, you can cook what you want for supper, put the kettles in the fireless cooker, and attend to other things, or go out, without the slightest anxiety, and at supper time find it hot and deliciously cooked.

You can cook the oatmeal, or any cereal for 5 minutes after supper, put it in the fireless cooker, and find it thoroughly cooked and hot at any time in the morning needed. You can cook a boiled dinner, on a hot summer day, without any odor or heat in your kitchen. All this can be done on a fireless cooker.

We give below a few directions for cooking with this new cooker, which will enable the beginner to avoid loss and worry by mistakes.

Baked Beans

Soak over night in cold water. In the morning drain and add two quarts of fresh water for each quart of beans, and a piece of salt pork; boil hard on coal or gas stove 10 or 15 minutes; remove quickly to cabinet for three or four hours; then take from cabinet and boil hard 10 minutes more and return to cabinet for three or four hours longer; pour into bake dish and brown in oven.

Soups

Prepare in usual way; boil five or ten minutes; remove to cabinet for 3 or 4 hours. Water in which meats have been boiled, with proper seasoning and chopped up vegetables, makes excellent soups.

Cereals

Measure into your granite kettle, water required, salt to taste, stir in your cereal slowly and boil 5 minutes. Remove to cabinet for 3 or 4 hours or over night.

Oat Flakes. – 1 cup oats to 3 cups water. Leave 4 hours or more.
Oatmeal. — 1 cup oats to 4 of water, 4 hours or more.
Cream of Wheat. – 1 cup wheat, 6 of water, 4 hours or more.
Cornmeal Mush. – 1 cup meal, 4 cups water, 4 hours or more.
Boiled Rice. – 1 cup rice, 5 water or milk, 2 hours or more.

Vegetables (Boiled)

Prepare in usual way, put into large kettle, cover with water; bring to a boil on coal or gas stove and boil hard 5 minutes; remove quickly to cabinet for two or three hours or more. Beets, turnips, carrots, hubbard squash or vegetables requiring a long time to cook, will be greatly improved if taken from cabinet after two or three hours, reheated for five or ten minutes and returned to cabinet for two or three hours longer. Potatoes if cut in two will cook nicely in one hour and a quarter. Potatoes with jackets on require three hours.

Boiled Meats

Put meat into kettle, cover with boiling water, boil hard 10 or 15 minutes; remove quickly to cabinet for 3 or 4 hours; then return to the stove and boil hard 5 or 10 minutes more and return to cabinet for 3 or 4 hours longer. Chicken and tender meats will not require the second heating. There is no danger from over-cooking. It is advisable to start cooking meats for mid-day meal the night before; leave in cabinet over night, and give it the second boiling in the morning; for supper start in the morning, re-heat at noon. For boiling dinner, put the vegetables in the kettle with the meat at the second boiling. Always be sure that water is boiling hard when kettle is placed in cabinet.

Roast Meats

Sear meat in hot skillet or spider; put it in the small granite pail with two cups of hot water for gravy; roast in hot oven 15 or 20 minutes. While meat is roasting, put two or three quarts of water in one of the large kettles and bring to a boil. Remove pail containing roast from oven and place on rack in large kettle, surrounded by boiling water; boil hard 5 or 10 minutes, remove quickly to cabinet for 3 or 4 hours. Cover should be on small pail; this is not necessary if roast is large. A small roast will not require as much cooking as a large one. The liquid in small pail may be thickened with flour if desired for gravy. If the meat is tough, start cooking in the evening, leave in the cabinet over night; in the morning reheat kettle for 10 minutes and return to cabinet until noon; or if wanted for supper start cooking in the morning and reheat at noon.

Boston Brown Bread

Mix one cup of wheat flour, one cup cornmeal, one cup of rye or graham flour, one teaspoon salt, two teaspoons soda; then add one cup sour milk, three-fourths cup molasses. Pour into a small pail about three-fourths full. Place on rack in large kettle surrounded with boiling water. Boil on flame stove 20 minutes. Remove to cabinet for 5 hours or more. By adding half cup of raisins, you have fruit bread.

Vegetables (Steamed)

Place vegetables in cheesecloth bag; insert cover of large kettle into mouth of bag; draw up shirr string and the bow-knot; fill bottle one-third full of water; put cover in position. The vegetables will then hang beneath the cover and above the water. Bring to a boil and boil hard 10 minutes; remove quickly to cabinet for time required for boiling vegetables.

Boiled Fish

Roll fish in cheesecloth and tie the ends; lower into kettle of boiling water; boil on stove 5 or 10 minutes. Remove to cabinet for 3 or 4 hours.

Dried Fruit

Soak over night in cold water. Boil on flame stove 5 or 10 minutes. Remove to cabinet for 4 or 5 hours.

Sweeten to taste.

Steamed Graham Bread

Mix three cups graham flour, one cup flour, one teaspoon salt, three teaspoons soda, one cup molasses, two and one-half cups sour milk. Cook same as Boston Brown Bread.

NOTE---For steaming vegetables a cheesecloth bag can easily be made with shirr string. An ordinary steamer can be used to steam meats or bread, or a special kettle for use in Fireless Cookers, is now carried by some of the large hardware firms. Whenever it is necessary to prepare food in less time than is required in the directions, take the kettle out of the cooker after it has been in one-half the time in which you have to cook in, and boil hard on a stove for five minutes; then put back into the cooker until time to serve. By so doing the cooking can be done in the cooker about as quickly as on a stove. Ordinarily food should be left in the cooker at least twice as long as it takes to cook it on the stove. This is not an objectionable feature, as there is no fuel consumed and the secret of good cooking is slow and thorough cooking.

TIME TABLE FOR COOKING

Vegetables	Boil on Stove Minutes	Leave in Fireless Stove Hours
Potatoes	5	2
Peas, green	5	2
Tomatoes	5	2
Corn, green	5	3
Onions	10	3
Cabbage	10	3
String beans	10	3
Turnips	15	4
Beets, green	15	2
Cereals		
Oatmeal	2	All Night
Tapioca	5	2
Sago	5	2
Rice	5	2
Puddings		
Drop Dumplings	5	2
Cottage	10	3
Fruit Dumplings	10	3
Suet	30	4
Meats		
Veal, 2 lbs	15	3
Fish, 2 lbs	15	2
Beef, 2 lbs	15	3
Chicken, spring	15	3
Beef, 3 lbs	30	4
Ham, 3 lbs	30	all day
Pork, 2 lbs	30	4
Chicken, 1 yr	30	4
Corned beef	30	4
Pork, 3 lbs	35	4

THIS AND THAT

So-called catering with a Dutch oven

If you hear of someone who caters, Dutch oven style, for large gatherings, you may be amazed and overwhelmed by the idea. I know because I was. I heard about a person who was going to cook for about 250 people. One of the few times in my life I was speechless. My first thought was what a Dutch oven master this person had to be. He needed at least 6 arms and hundreds of pounds of charcoal briquettes. I couldn't imagine just one person doing all the work. This was a chance of a lifetime for such a learning experience. Needless to say, I could hardly wait to meet such a person. I ventured forth and introduced myself. He looked like any other person and I couldn't help but wonder how he could manage such a feat by himself. After talking to him a few minutes I offered my labor in exchange for the learning experience and a great meal. He accepted my offer but the big day was still a few weeks away. I was like a child waiting for Christmas morning. I could hardly contain myself thinking about everything that I was going to learn. However, like I said, the big cooking day was still weeks away. I marked my calendar and waited.

Finally the big day arrived. I awoke early, got ready and arrived ready to work. Then my whole bubble burst. The day went sort of like this. We cut the vegetables for a green salad. We started two cobblers, for dessert, in camp Dutch ovens using hot coals on top and bottom. The rest of the meal consisted of baked beans; a chicken and rice dish and store bought potato rolls. The baked beans and chicken and rice were cooked in Dutch ovens on a propane gas stove. The salad came from a bag and we added a few tomatoes. The chicken came from the frozen food section of the store. The beans came from a can.

Nothing was cooked at the location but was made to appear as such. The Dutch ovens with the cobbler were transported and set up, with the briquettes. The other Dutch ovens were set up on a table to be used as serving dishes.

I watch with interest, as those being served were truly delighted at tasting a dinner, which they believed to be a truly old-fashioned cooked Dutch oven meal. Many thought and were led to believe the meal had been cooked in the ground.

I don't write this to demean or hurt all those people who cater with Dutch ovens. I write it to reveal the fact that not all you hear about Master Dutch oven cooks is true. This is also by way of encouragement to those of you who may feel to master this art of cooking is left only to a few. With good instruction, time and practice, you too could be catering dinners with Dutch ovens and you need not rely on gas to do the job.

The Golden Dutch

My family has lived in and around, what is now called Caldwell, Idaho, since 1864. In 1864 it was Idaho Territory and there was no town of Caldwell for another 19 years. The wagon train had left Missouri on May 10, 1864, with a destination of Oregon, and arrived in this area, September 2, 1864. The trek had been a long, hot and exhausting trip over the dry plains of heat, dust and rocks. The wagon train had started with a large number of wagons but when it arrived at Fort Hall, in southeastern Idaho, the greater portion of families decided to go to California. It was a hot August and crossing the Idaho desert created many hardships, including typhoid, for the pioneers.

My great great-grandfather, Reuben Cox, was wagon master and he was very ill with typhoid. The train passed through Boise, which consisted of a few buildings and tents. They followed the river towards Oregon. About 30 miles west of Boise they rounded a bend in the river and arrived at what was actually the highest point in the area. They were sick, tired and completely exhausted. They looked out over the river and saw a sight, which looked like Paradise to them. They could see for miles and there was the river winding through lush green trees, bushes and grass. (Even today a person can go up on Canyon Hill and see the same scene as my ancestors saw in 1864.) Reuben Cox decided the wagon train would rest for a while before going to Oregon.

As soon as Reuben started feeling better, one by one each of his children came down with typhoid. Anna, wife of Reuben, nursed her family back to health and was fortunate not to come down with typhoid herself. Then on Jan. 23, 1865, she gave birth to a girl. (This was really a pioneer woman.) The family arrived too late in the year to build a cabin and had to live in their covered wagon and a tent. A few miles away was a cabin, which had been built earlier in the year by Dave and Tom Johnston. Another brother, Dennis, was fighting the Civil War. The winter 1864-65 was one of the most severe known to the early pioneers. There was about two feet of snow that came in the early part of winter and remained till the following March. When a member of the Cox family reached a point where they could be moved, Dave and Tom Johnston welcomed the person into their own cabin and took care of them. (Their cabin stands in the Caldwell Memorial Park today.)

The three Johnston brothers were well known in the area and made a great contribution to its settlement. There was another brother, Hardy Richard Johnston, who was my great great-grandfather. David, Thomas and Dennis never married and lived in their small cabin for 52 years. Each brother homesteaded a piece of land and purchased more land till they had 640 acres and they prospered over the years. They engaged principally in the cattle business and they also grew grain. Some referred to them as the wealthiest individuals in the area. They enjoyed the simple life, devoid of haste, worry or the yearning for so-called luxuries. The brothers had orderly lives. Each brother had his own job to do whether working on the ranch or doing household chores. All three helped with the cooking. It is said after the meal was cooked in the Dutch oven, they would place it in the middle of the table and each brother would help himself. Each brother had mastered Dutch oven cooking at a very early age. Some of the early pioneers said they were the best cooks in the valley and there wasn't anything they couldn't cook in their Dutch oven.

They had bank accounts but they wanted to make sure their future was secure so they also kept money at home. This was probably a habit which was formed before there were banks in the area. They hid their gold coins in cans or whatever they had to use. One of their nephews stole some coins. He was not the smartest thief because he went to town and made a few purchases such as new clothes, gun and holster and a nice new saddle. Then he went to proudly show his family the nice things he had bought. It didn't take long for the family to figure out what he had done and was disowned by his parents and uncles. His picture, which hung on the wall, was turned over to face the wall. It was such a disgrace he left the area and to this day no one has any idea what became of him.

When my uncle was about six years of age, his family was visiting his great uncles and they sent him to a shed to get something. (When he told me the story he said it had happened so long ago he forgot what he was sent to get for them.) He was told it was in a container on the shelf. He said there was a lot of junk in that old shed but there was also gold coins. He found junk, like nuts, bolts,

Dennis, left, Tom, center and David Johnston relax in front of their cabin near Caldwell, Idaho, in this photograph taken before 1909. The Johnston brothers were the first settlers in the area, homesteading in 1865. The Johnston cabin is now in the Caldwell City Park.

nails and even dirt, in the cans but under that junk he found gold coins. It wasn't just one or two cans, gold was found in all the cans. Then he found it! There on the floor sat an Old Dutch oven just waiting for him to open it. As in the other containers there was a lot of junk, but under that junk he found more gold coins, about two inches deep. The Dutch oven was very old and had seen a lot of use. It was probably the one the Johnstons brought with them when they arrived in 1864. It was rusted and no longer used for cooking. It's cooking days were over and now was used to hold their gold. My uncle said he was so frightened they would find him looking at the gold, he hurried to put back everything and ran back to their cabin, telling no one what he had found. On the way home, he told his family about The Golden Dutch Oven and everything he had seen. His father related a story to him about how Dave, Dennis and Tom not only hid gold in whatever container was available but they also hid gold on their land under rocks and sagebrush. They would find a rock, dig a hole under it and stash some gold and marked the spot with sagebrush.

This worked well for the three brothers, when they were younger. In order to find a place for their gold, they had to go farther from their cabin to find a rock they had not used. As they got older, they failed to tell each other where they had hidden the gold and they became very forgetful, but kept hiding gold.

David died first, November 3, 1916. His brother Tom was next and died on January 17, 1920. On May 29, 1922 Dennis died. The estate was divided among the surviving relatives. A lot of time was spent trying to find all their gold. After awhile the property was sold and the story is told, the man who bought the land could be seen plowing the land both day and night but never planted a crop. To this day no one knows if he ever found gold.

And what happened to The Golden Dutch? That also remains a mystery.

DUTCH OVEN TERMINOLOGY

BAKING MIX: A multi purpose mix. A mix for making such items as biscuits, pancakes and waffles.

BLANCH: Bring water to a boil then immerse vegetables for 3 minutes. This will replace steaming vegetables while using a Dutch oven.

BLEND: Mix together the ingredients.

BLOOM: Describes what happens after any yeast dough rises and is ready to be baked. As an example, when bread, in a Dutch, is set over hot coals the heat will cause the bread to expand, or bloom, a little. This applies to any and all yeast items.

BOIL: Heat liquid to a temperature (boiling point) at which vapor rises. When liquid reaches the boiling point, it will not get hotter. It is best to cook at a slow boil. Using a rolling boil will not cook any faster but will cause the vegetables to break apart giving you poor results.

BROWN: Using a medium high heat, with oil or butter in your Dutch, put the meat in the Dutch and sear on all sides. This not only adds color to the meat but adds a great deal of flavor. This also locks in the juice of the meat making it tender.

BROIL: Works the same way as the broiler in your oven of a household stove. You pile all the hot coals on the Dutch lid in order to finish the item you are cooking.

COAL LIGHTER: Same as chimney

CHIMNEY: A metal tube-shaped object with a handle designed especially for starting your briquettes without using lighter liquid. You put paper on the bottom with the briquettes on top. Light the paper and let stand till briquettes are ready to use.

CREAM: Mix ingredients until there is a creamy texture.

DE-GLAZE: To de-glaze a Dutch means to use a wooden spoon and scrape the bottom of the Dutch and use the scrapings to make gravy.

DEVELOP: Mixing yeast dough to the point where the dough is elastic and shiny. Stretch the dough thin and it should be transparent when pulled or stretched.

EGG WASH: A mixture of 1 part egg and 2 parts cold water then whip together. This is used as a top wash or a help to stick dough together. Used in various ways such as sticking together the edge of the top and bottom crust of pies, wash over top of pie to add color, wash over top of cinnamon rolls and etc.

KNEAD: The mixing of any yeast raised dough by hand after the flour has absorbed the liquid. The process of kneading develops the gluten in the flour necessary to hold the gas made by the yeast feeding on the sugar and milk solids. This process will cause the dough to rise. Use the heal of your hand to knead the dough.

LID LIFTER: An item made especially for removing the lid from the Dutch oven. You can use a claw hammer; it will work quite well.

LID HOLDER: Same as lid stand.

LID STAND: An item made especially for setting a hot Dutch lid on when cooking. To be used to hold your lid while stirring the Dutch. Also used to hold Dutch lid upside down when using lid as a fry pan.

LOAD THE LID: To heat only the lid of the Dutch oven. (See preheat below.)

MARINADE: The liquid used to marinate meat.

MARINATE: A process that allows the seasoned liquid to penetrate the food to change the flavor. Use with meat or vegetables. You cover the item with the marinade and put in a covered container.

MEALY: A stage in mixing when the ingredients are soft and smooth to touch, having the quality of meal, particularly size of wheat.

PAINT: Refers to painting the tops of cinnamon rolls, bread, biscuits and dinner rolls with an egg wash, butter or milk to add color to the top of the item.

PREHEAT: To heat the Dutch or Dutch lid before attempting to cook or bake. To preheat the lid you place hot coals on lid before the lid is placed on the Dutch. This is done in order to have an instant top heat on the Dutch.

PROOF: The rising of any item with yeast after it had been placed in the final baking pan. Such items are bread, dinner rolls and cinnamon rolls. If the bread dough is allowed to proof too high, with no room for it to bloom in the Dutch oven, it will fall back; meaning it was over proofed.

RISE: After the yeast dough is mixed, put it into a bowl and let it rise (double in size). After it has doubled, remove it from the bowl and round the dough into a ball. Place the dough on a floured surface and let it rise again until doubled in size. Then shape the dough to fit size of bread pan as in the modern style of Dutch oven baking or round the dough into a ball and place directly into the Dutch as in the old style Dutch oven baking. The next step is letting the dough double in size again and the final rise is called proofing the dough.

ROUND UP: To form the bread dough into a ball with your hands.

SEAR: Heat oil in a Dutch in order to brown meat fast over a high heat. Brown meat on one side then the other. On a thick piece of meat also brown the other four sides.

SIMMER: Bring to a slow boil. Use simmering for such things as stews soups, chili or pot roast.

STACKING: When you stack one Dutch oven on top of another which enables you to cook 2 or more items at the same time.

TRIVET: A small wire rack, with legs, to use in the bottom of the Dutch to hold the food from direct contact with the Dutch. Use a trivet when baking bread, rolls or pies using the modern style of Dutch baking. A trivet is also useful when roasting beef, turkey, ham or chicken when a small amount of water is used. A trivet should hold food at least 1/2 inch from the bottom of the Dutch. In place of a trivet some cooks will use 3 to 4 canning jar rings. The rings will work fine when baking the modern style, however, when roasting with water, in time the varnish will come off the rings and into whatever you are cooking. I recommend using a stainless steel or a cast iron trivet.

TRUSS: A process used to secure the legs and wings of a bird (chicken, turkey) while cooking. **Always use 100 percent cotton string.** Wrap the string around the wings and legs to hold them in place while cooking. You may use bamboo skewers to hold the cavities of the bird in place while cooking. Wrapping the string around the skewers, wings and legs is the best way of trussing a bird for cooking.

HERBS FOR FLAVOR AND FRAGRANCE

ALL SPICE – use in soup, stew, pot roast, sauces, marinades and preserves

BASIL – use with eggs, beef dishes, pork dishes and fish dishes – good in any recipe using tomatoes

BAY LEAVES – use in stew, soups, pot roast or when cooking vegetables

CARAWAY SEED – use in rye bread – when ground it gives rye bread a better flavor

CARDAMON – use in sweet breads such as cinnamon rolls or Danish rolls – a great flavoring

CAYENNE – use in chili, soup, stew, dips, spreads, eggs dishes, barbecue sauce, guacamole and meat dishes

CHILI POWDER – use in many Mexican dishes such as chili, tamales and enchiladas, great in tomato or barbecue sauces, adds flavor to meat load and hamburgers

CHIVES – use where mild onion flavor is required

CINNAMON - best known for use in pastries such as cinnamon rolls and cinnamon bread, use in cakes, pies and puddings

CLOVES – use in soups, stews, pot roast, cakes and cookies

COREANDER – candies, meat dishes, pudding—ground seeds used in baking

CUMIN – a must for Mexican dishes such as Spanish rice, tamales, enchiladas and refried beans

GARLIC – used in sauces, soups, spaghetti, meats, stir fry and breads

GINGER - use in oriental stir-fry and in baking items and some meats and vegetables

LEMON PEEL – use in place of true lemon flavor, use in pastries, pudding, icing, cakes and cookies

MACE - use in pastries, pies, cakes, doughnuts, quick breads, custard, and pudding

MARJORAM – "sweet" use with meat, fish and poultry also tomato sauce, spaghetti, pizza and salad

NUTMEG – use in same dishes as Mace

MUSTARD – use in meat loaf, sandwiches, ham glaze, potato salad, deviled eggs, sauces and hamburger

ONION – the use of onions, yellow, red or green are to numerous to mention – stir-fry, meat loaf, soup, stew, salads, pot roast, hamburgers and some gravies

OREGANO – use in spaghetti sauce, Mexican dishes, pizza, dishes with tomatoes and some meat dishes with fish, fowl, lamb and pork

PAPKRIKA – use to both flavor and color foods, use with chicken, fish and barbecued meats

PARSLEY – use in salads, meats, soups and for garnish

PEPPER – next to salt, pepper is used more than any other seasoning – season to taste

PEPPERCORNS – the whole black pepper before it is cracked or ground – use in soups, stews and meat dishes, usually removed before serving

POULTRY SEASONING – used to season chicken stock, roast chicken or turkey and dressing (stuffing)

RED PEPPER – same as cayenne

ROSEMARY – add to meats, poultry and eggs

SAGE – use in stuffing, sausage, lamb, pork and poultry

SEASON ALL – used to season all meat lamb, pork, poultry, beef and fish

SHALLOTS – leaves are used like chives, it has a mild onion flavor

TARRAGON – use with fish, poultry, shellfish and salad dressings

THYME – use lightly with all meats and wild game

Crush all dried seasonings between fingers, before adding to any dish. This will enhance the flavor and aroma of the seasonings.

RECIPE INDEX

THE AUTHOR

Dale I. Smith was born in his grandmother's home on Canyon Hill in Caldwell, Idaho. He grew up and attended school in Caldwell. As a youth, Dale spent a lot of time with his family camping, fishing and hunting in the Idaho mountains and he learned the importance of good food on those occasions. Members of his family were all excellent cooks and Dale followed their examples.

After spending some time in the Navy, Dale returned to Caldwell and started his baking career. In 1959 he married Alice Witzig and they have two sons, Bryan and Steven.

In 1966 and 1967 Dale worked for a food service organization in South Vietnam, baking and cooking for the Air Force. After returning to the states, Dale owned and operated a bakery in northern California until the family returned to Idaho. For the next twelve years he was president and business agent for the local Bakery and Confectionery Workers Union. He retired in 1990 to enjoy the Idaho outdoors and to perfect his Dutch Oven cooking techniques.

Other cookbooks
From CAXTON PRESS

Rocky Mountain Wild Foods Cookbook
ISBN 0-87004-367-6
6 x 9, 250 pages, illustrations $17.95

Basque Cooking and Lore
ISBN 0-87004-346-3
6x9, illustrations, maps,
175 pages, $14.95

Sowbelly and Sourdough
ISBN 0-87004-369-2
6x9, 167 pages, $14.95

The Complete Sourdough Cookbook
ISBN 0-87004-223-8
6x9, 136 pages, illustrations, $12.95

Don Holm's Book of Food Drying, Pickling & Smoke Curing
ISBN 0-87004-250-5
6x9, 131 pages, illustrations, $17.95

Old-Fashioned Dutch Oven Cookbook
ISBN 0-87004-133-9
6x9, 131 pages, illustrations, $14.95

Matt Braun's Western Cooking
ISBN 0-87004-374-9
8 x 8 185 pages, illustrations, $17.95

For a free Caxton catalog write to:

CAXTON PRESS
312 Main Street
Caldwell, ID 83605-3299

or

Visit our Internet Website:

www.caxtonpress.com

Caxton Press is a division of The CAXTON PRINTERS, Ltd.